THE *Eucharist* AND SOCIAL JUSTICE

Margaret Scott

Paulist Press
New York/Mahwah, NJ

Imprimi Potest: Sister Sagrario Nuñez, acj, provincial, United States province, Handmaids of the Sacred Heart of Jesus
March 23, 2008
Philadelphia, Pennsylvania

Cover and book design by Lynn Else

Library of Congress Cataloging-in-Publication Data
Scott, Margaret, 1942–
    The Eucharist and social justice / Margaret Scott.
      p. cm.
    Includes bibliographical references (p.   ).
    ISBN 978-0-8091-4566-9 (alk. paper)
    1. Lord's Supper—Catholic Church. 2. Christianity and justice—Catholic Church. 3. Poverty—Religious aspects—Catholic Church. 4. Catholic Church—Doctrines. I. Title.
    BX2215.3.S36 2009
    234'.163—dc22

                        2008053809

Published by Paulist Press
997 Macarthur Boulevard
Mahwah, New Jersey 07430

www.paulistpress.com

Printed and bound in the
United States of America

Contents

This book is dedicated to my religious family, the Handmaids of the Sacred Heart of Jesus. The Handmaids have enabled my two passions: Jesus Christ in the Eucharist, and the poor. I fell in love with the Eucharistic Christ as a college student, in the order's convent chapel in London, England. Later, as a Handmaid, they gave me the opportunity of traveling widely in Africa and Asia, and then living and working in South America, where my love affair with the poor began.

Preface

We were behind a garbage truck as it rumbled its way out of Quito toward Chilibulo. It was our first visit to Ecuador, my first trip to South America. The truck stopped at a vast landfill on the outskirts of the Ecuadoran capital to disgorge its load of trash from the restaurants and upper-market area of Quito. I watched with horror as the mountains of trash began to heave with activity. I presumed it was hordes of scavenging dogs. But it was *people*—crowds of hungry men, women, and children frantically burrowing in other people's trash for food, for yesterday's bread.

Chilibulo left a lasting impression on me. I had seen, with my own eyes, that in our world today there are some who have a great deal and others, many others, who have nothing at all. Some eat more than enough food today, and every day—enough to throw yesterday's leftovers into the trash where others, who have no food today, will find it tomorrow.

The Eucharist and Social Justice is, in part, autobiographical. It is about my passion for the Eucharist and my passion for the poor. It is based on my personal eucharistic story, as a member of a religious congregation centered in the Eucharist,[1] and on the privileged experience of being befriended by the poor in many contexts and in many places: India, Philippines, South and Central America, the United States, Europe, and Africa. I moved into the field of international relations and lectured to university commerce students on globalization and the poor. Drawing on my experience and research, I wanted to bring my two loves together.

Doing so has raised many basic questions for me. Is there something in the dynamic of the eucharistic celebration that can inform globalization and make it more humane, inclusive, and sustainable? Does the Eucharist offer a paradigm for sharing the earth's goods and building community? Can it provide a language that can be used by institutions and men and women of goodwill to address the alleviation of poverty? Can it enable the poor to make globalization "work" for them too? Whatever happened to the heartbeat of Christ in the Eucharist, pulsating with special love for the poor and the powerless? Can our eucharistic celebrations overflow with a passion for justice? How do we make our eucharistic celebrations more alive and relevant, more about real people and not reduced to a private, spiritual experience, lost in rubrics?

The early Church, in its own socioeconomic and political context, acknowledged an inseparable relationship between the Eucharist and the poor is its eucharistic practice. Well known is St. Paul's scathing indictment of the Christians in Corinth, who gathered for the Eucharist but left the poor without food, who confessed the presence of Christ in the consecrated host but ignored him in the hungry. The same intuition is found in the *Didache* and the *Didascalia Apostolorum*, and in the writings of many of the fathers of the Church, some of whom went as far as to say that the poor were the altar on which the Eucharist is celebrated.[2] But somehow, since then, we have lost the eucharistic imagination expressed so well by St. Irenaeus: "Our manner of thinking is conformed to the Eucharist and the Eucharist confirms our manner of thinking."[3]

Over the centuries, liturgical reform and the development of the social doctrine of the Church seem to have moved forward on parallel tracks, coming together only briefly in the insights of the liturgical movement in Louvain in the 1930s, which saw liturgy as an indispensable basis for social regeneration—an insight that inspired Virgil Michael's work in the United States. Even Vatican II's *Gaudium et Spes* and *Sacrosanctum Concilium* fail to make an explicit connection between the Eucharist and social justice. In the 1980s a few authors on different continents *did* begin making that connection but their voices faded away.

Now, twenty-plus-years on, it seems a matter of urgency to recapture the early Christian tradition and restore that nexus between the Eucharist and the poor in the twenty-first century, an epoch characterized by globalization. There are two reasons that give immediacy to my own writing.

I began writing in 2005, the year designated by John Paul II as the Year of the Eucharist—a year that provided a locus for all those who think about and who celebrate Eucharist to *reimagine* Eucharist. This was an opportunity to rediscover in the Eucharist a theological basis for the social doctrine of the Church and to discover the potential of the Eucharist as a hermeneutical key to globalization.

The year 2005 also witnessed a growing consensus worldwide about the alleviation of poverty. The Make Poverty History campaign, launched in the United Kingdom, wanted 2005 to be remembered as "the year that changed the world."[4] We also saw World in Hunger, a campaign to save humanity, which met in Jordan immediately prior to the World Economic Forum in May 2005. Economists also weighed in with books on the same theme: Jeffrey Sachs' *The End of Poverty* and Petra Rivoli's *The Travels of a T-Shirt in the Global Economy*. Using a series of worldwide Live 8 concerts, given "this time not for charity but for political justice,"[5] rock stars and rock groups, too, attempted to raise public awareness and pressure the Group of Eight, or G8—a forum of the leading industrial nations—to do more to lift Africa out of poverty.

I continued writing *The Eucharist and Social Justice* in 2006, which opened with *Time* Magazine naming three Good Samaritans as "Persons of the Year": Bill and Melinda Gates, and rock star Bono, describing them as "three people on a global mission to end poverty, disease—and indifference...."[6] In the year 2006, many Oscars went to "social issues,"[7] films about homosexuality and racism, corruption and corporate crime—all of them movies with "a message for social change";[8] and in 2006, Francis Fukuyama's book *America at the Crossroads*[9] revised his earlier opinion[10] that liberal democracy is the culmination of humankind's ideological development, substituting a foreign policy characterized by economic development and foreign aid.

The Eucharist and Social Justice was finally finished in 2007, just after Pope Benedict XVI's postsynodal exhortation on the Eucharist, *Sacramentum Caritatis*, was promulgated.

In such a climate, the "adventure" of the Eucharist is *not* just for Catholics but for a much bigger constituency. It can take on the dimensions that God intended for it: the life of the world. It can provide a paradigm for sharing the world's goods and building community for everyone. It can offer a strategy and a language that can be used by institutions and men and women of good will to address the alleviation of poverty. Therefore, *The Eucharist and Social Justice* is written for all those who want to make the world a better place, for the growing coalition of the caring. It is a book for believers and nonbelievers alike, for people of all creeds and people of none, for the young and the not-so-young.

Even though the Eucharist is one organic, all-embracing act, and not disconnected moments, one following the other, the main movements of the eucharistic celebration can provide a structure to explore some of the many different dimensions of the relationship between Eucharist and social justice. I have chosen seven of those powerfully dynamic movements to suggest that the Eucharist is deeply political and potentially subversive. I also make ample use of the eucharistic texts, which are pregnant with meaning and embrace a whole host of issues around poverty.

PREFACE

The Eucharist is about inclusivity, and is both a protest and resistance to social exclusion. The Eucharist is where liturgy and life interact. It is about real people who, nourished by the Word of God that is broken and shared, incarnate that Word in the here and now, in a particular historical and cultural context. The Eucharist challenges the agricultural subsidies and unfair trade practices of the richer nations. It is a statement about sweatshops and about land issues. It speaks to the exploitation of the planet. The Eucharist offers a counter-narrative: an alternative way of looking at history, one at odds with the widely and uncritically accepted pack of corporate myths and political half-truths crafted by the rich and powerful. It presents, rather, the story of humanity as read through the eyes of the poor. The Eucharist is about solidarity and sharing. It initiates reflection and fosters dialogue about community. Embedded in Eucharist are issues around discrimination, vulnerability, and violence. Finally, the Eucharist is dynamic: it empowers action and it enables us to make a difference.

The Eucharist and Social Justice is by no means intended to be an exhaustive conversation around the Eucharist. That would be impossible. The Eucharist is a deep, bottomless well: there is always more and more to it, countless dimensions to explore, many hidden depths to discover and to share. I have spent the last forty years drinking from that well and feel that I have, as yet, merely skimmed the surface. Clearly, I am talking about the Eucharist as it is meant to be, as it can be. In practice, that does not always happen in our weekly or even daily eucharistic celebrations. Different philosophical considerations and theological emphases, together with a concern for externals, have sometimes separated the liturgy from life and succeeded in making the eucharistic celebrations somewhat irrelevant and the amazing riches and power that the Eucharist embraces seem somehow lost in a maze of rubrics.

I thank my congregation, the Handmaids of the Sacred Heart of Jesus, for gifting me with the time and the space to write;

Gap LoBiondo, SJ., and the Woodstock Theological Center, Georgetown University, for facilitating my research and for their encouragement; the Visitation Sisters, Georgetown, for giving me a home, their prayers, and loving support; and Rev. Lawrence Boadt, CSP, for his encouragement and generous acceptance of my manuscript, which he described as "an excellent reflection and a teaching book on the connection between the Eucharist and social justice." Thank you to all those who have been a part of *The Eucharist and Social Justice*. Above all, my thanks go to the very many poor people the world over, who have touched my life and made me a more eucharistic woman.

Chapter One

"The Lord Be with You"

"San Romero de El Salvador. San Romero de América Latina. San Romero del Mundo. ¡Viva!"[1]

In a growing awareness of inclusivity and catholicity, thousands of voices echoed across the Plaza del Salvador del Mundo in the city of San Salvador during the eucharistic celebration to commemorate the 25th anniversary of the assassination of Archbishop Oscar Romero. Voices embodied in the vast congregation gathered in the square.

Everyone was there. The famous—the Jon Sobrinos and the Samuel Ruizes—and the unknown; theologians and simple, Spirit-filled people of God; prelates of the universal Church and God's priestly people gathered from every corner of the earth—from Africa, Asia, Europe, South, Central and North America. There were the rich and the poor; aristocrats and peasants; the sister of the presumed "intellectual author" of the murder of Romero, standing side by side with a *campesino*, a farmer, who held a poster depicting the faces of a hundred other martyrs. There were indigenous peoples in their native costumes mingling with the well-dressed social elite. There were men, women, and children and, above all, young people—lots of them, Catholics and non-Catholics alike. God's people, God's family.

Standing there among them gave me an overwhelming sense of the identity of a eucharistic community and of the globality and inclusivity that underlies every eucharistic celebration.

The Identity of the Eucharistic Community

In many places today, as in El Salvador, the Catholic eucharistic community is a multiethnic, multicultural, and multilingual throng gathered around the "table of the world," giving color, texture, and song to the eucharistic celebration.

At the same time, the eucharistic community is made up of real people, each one with his or her own personal story that sets the Eucharist—every Eucharist—in the context of the here and now, integrating into the Eucharist the basic elements that make up our everyday lives and the burning issues that affect the men and women of our time: food and drink, hunger and survival, work and celebration, economics and the use of power. The Christ whom we encounter in the Eucharist meets us in and through the structures of historical existence: matter, time, space, language, community, culture, and social, economic, and political relationships.

The Eucharist, then, is part of the flow of life. More than that, it has an impact on daily life, and the daily life of the eucharistic community has an impact on the Eucharist. Hence, "the Eucharist should have the dimension that God meant for it: the life of the world."[2] The eucharistic community can make that happen. It gathers for the Eucharist to celebrate what it is and what it lives. It disperses after the Eucharist to be and to live what it celebrates.

SAINTS AND SINNERS

The eucharistic community is made up of people, real people who are both saints and sinners. Those who care deeply, and those who could care more. Those who struggle for their own survival and those who fight for the survival of others. Those who see God and those who are groping to find him. Those who are broken and those who are whole. The eucharistic community in the Plaza del Salvador mirrored the brokenness of our fractured world in both the Salvadoran textile worker who receives thirty-three cents an hour and in the white South African bishop who spent most of his life resisting apartheid. It is about broken people who are also complicit in the brokenness of our world. It is about the globalizers and the globalized; those who dictate tariffs and quotas, who grant subsidies and impose free trade. It is also about those who cannot compete in the world marketplace. There is room for all around the table—for those whom we expect to meet seated at the table, with whom we feel comfortable, and for those whose presence is inconvenient, rather unsettling, and even shocking. Everyone.

PRIESTS AND PROPHETS

The eucharistic community is also made up of both priests and prophets.

The Church tells us that we are priests with a baptismal priesthood. We are God's Spirit-filled people "consecrated to be…a holy priesthood";[3] a "royal priesthood of believers"[4] with a Spirit-given power to gather and celebrate the memory of Christ. While believing wholeheartedly in the ministerial priesthood, we know that the eucharistic community is the "subject of the liturgical action," not recipients of it or passive spectators in mere attendance, waiting to stand in line to receive communion.[5] For the liturgy is the action of the whole Christ and so the whole community celebrates and offers it along with the priest-celebrant. The whole community is called to what Vatican II described as a "full, active and conscious participation" in the liturgy[6] or, in the words of the early fathers, called to be "true adorers and true priests."[7]

Greek Orthodox theology, in the early biblical-patristic tradition, adds an anthropological perspective to our priestly identity. It sees all human beings as intrinsically eucharistic, created by God for loving communion with him through the gift of food: "See, I have given you every plant yielding seed that is upon the face of all the earth, and every tree with seed in its fruit; you shall have them for food."[8] Man and woman, in receiving this "divine love made food," give God thanks and praise.[9] In this Byzantine vision, humanity's initial response to the gift of life—food and communion with God—is that of thanksgiving. The Eucharist is essentially about life, food, and communion, while the very word *Eucharist* means "thanksgiving." So human beings were created to be priests of a primordial Eucharist, receiving life through creation and offering it back to God in an act of thanksgiving. Alexander Schmemann takes this thought a step further when he says: "The world was created as the 'matter,' the material of one all-embracing Eucharist, and man was created as the priest of this cosmic sacrament."[10]

We are also prophets. God's prophetic people in the Plaza del Salvador punctuated the eucharistic celebration with a chanted refrain: "*Queremos obispos, al lado de los pobres*" ("We want bishops who side with the poor"). They were speaking as prophets in the school of Oscar Romero who in 1980 challenged both the United States administration to stop sending military aid, which was being used to repress the people. Two months later, he challenged his own government and military: "Brothers, you are from the same people; you are killing fellow Salvadorians....In the name of God, in the name of the suffering people, I ask you, I beg you, I command you: in the name of God, stop the repression."[11] The eucharistic community gathered in the plaza were prophets responding to the call of their assassinated pastor: "If they kill all the priests and the bishop too...each one of you must become God's microphone, each one of you must become a prophet." They were prophets who listen and speak in the power of the Spirit.

They were prophets, as are the members of every eucharistic community, engaged in the prophetic action that is the Eucharist, in the prophetic words and actions of Jesus at the Last Supper. The Eucharist as a prophetic action engenders a prophetic presence and a prophetic consciousness in the eucharistic community as we "do this" in his memory. It gives birth to prophets who are energized in their ministry by the epiclesis to speak with a prophetic voice in the shaping of society, embodying Jesus' cry that is echoed in the cry of the poor who plead for global justice, for a humanity of diversified communion, formed in justice and peace. The Eucharist is a prophetic act to be continued in the life of those who celebrate it by *being* Eucharist, by *being* the Body of Christ. The Eucharist is a prophetic statement about the pain-filled, divided, and broken world in which we live, a pointer to what the future could be: global solidarity, humanity reconciled. The Eucharist celebrates, in anticipation, God's dream for his world, for his people, come true.

A "TABLE-PEOPLE" AND
A HUNGRY PEOPLE

The eucharistic community gathers around a table to eat together. They are a hungry people, whether rich or poor. A people hungry for bread—our daily bread—and hungry for the Bread of Life; hungry for justice and for God and for the kingdom. Called to be the hungry people of the Beatitudes: "Blessed are they who hunger and thirst for righteousness, for they will be filled."[12] People hungry to break and share their bread with those who have no bread, with those who forage for yesterday's bread in the trash cans of the world: "The bread which they do not have convokes us, to be with You [Lord] their daily bread."[13]

Those who hunger for their daily bread, rice, or chapati are hungry, too, for a different bread, different from the fare that the global markets try to sell us; an alternative food like that which nourished Jesus: "I have food to eat that you do not know about."[14] A people hungry for the Eucharist like Jesus: "I have eagerly desired to eat this Passover with you before I suffer."[15] Like Jesus, who hungered to celebrate the miracle of his love and tenderness "made food" for us. A people hungry with an authentic desire: "that we might live no longer for ourselves."[16] Hungry for food for the journey toward the kingdom, for the nourishment to work for a better world, one in which poverty is, at last, made history.

The eucharistic community is also a "table-people" convoked by a God-Host who "can…spread a table in the wilderness"[17] and whose dream is to "make for all peoples a feast of rich food, a feast of well-matured wines."[18] A table-people who are gathered in the tradition of Jesus, who fed the crowds and who regularly ate with those on the margins of society, like prostitutes, tax-collectors, and sinners[19] and who insisted on welcoming to the table "the great unwashed…the shunned and the shamed,"[20] giving them a preferred place. A table-people who are true to the teaching of the early Christian community in which "no one claimed private ownership of any possessions, but everything they owned was held in common….There was not a needy person among them, for as many as owned land or houses sold them and brought the proceeds of what was sold. They laid them at the apostles' feet; and it was distributed to each as any had need."[21]

Like the early Christians, we are called to be a table-people who gather to create community: A community made up of equals. A community that can truly say: "At this table we put aside every worldly separation based on culture, class, or other differences….We no longer admit to distinctions based on age or sex or race or wealth,"[22] or on class or caste or disability—physical or mental. A community from which no one is excluded, not even those on the edges: the homeless, those with AIDS, the politically incorrect, the black sheep of the human family. A community with one heart and one soul. We are a table-people who become a community in the action of breaking and sharing bread; an action inextricably bound up with a burning concern that the poor and dispossessed should have enough to eat, for no other reason than that the Eucharist emphatically rejects all distinction between rich and poor.

GLOBAL AND INCLUSIVE

But each eucharistic community contains the whole Body of Christ, the whole Church. The local contains the universal. The community gathered for the Eucharist extends to embrace the pilgrim people of God, in all times and places. Wherever the Eucharist is celebrated, the whole Church is present—and the whole world, too. "The world is crucially present at the table, present in the story of suffering and death, present in the bread and wine taken from the earth, made by human hands, present in each person, each member of the body."[23] In other words, in the Eucharist "spatial and temporal divisions are collapsed" and we hold "the world in a wafer."[24]

The scope of the Eucharist is essentially global and inclusive. It is always richer and deeper, always more than we can ever imagine or dream. It is a prophetic word spoken and celebrated "from east to west,"[25] an action concerned with the "unity of the whole human race."[26] For that reason, the eucharistic community is *not* limited to the Catholic congregation gathered for Sunday Mass in a particular parish. It is a community that embraces "all God's children wherever they may be."[27]

The eucharistic community has never been just "us," the local community gathered for worship. We have always known that we have to leave room in the pews for "Blessed Mary, ever virgin, all the angels and saints," and "all the choirs of heaven." The patristic writings are replete with the vivid collapsing of spatial and temporal barriers at the Eucharist, to unite the whole Church on earth with the Church of all times and places and eternity. It is a community in the making, a community to come in the *eschaton*, the eschatological banquet. It is a community in anticipation of tomorrow. The eucharistic community reaches out beyond the Church to the world: from the temple into the street, and from the altar to all God's people.

In the same way, the issue of global hunger leads beyond the eucharistic table to embrace the whole human family. For the Eucharist is about eating together, about widening the tent and extending the table, making the table communal and therefore round—with no top and no bottom and no sides—a table as big as the whole world, a table for the eucharistic community that listens to the voices of those who seek food in their hunger, justice in their oppression, consolation in their pain, and reconciliation in their alienation.

The consecrated host is, literally and figuratively speaking, Jesus: the Jesus whose table-activity brought down and removed the walls of exclusion that limited attendance to the rich and the good. He left us, in inheritance, a table-fellowship with outcasts; an inclusive table-fellowship for all through the washing of the feet. The Host of the Last Supper is a God who wills that all people be saved. A God who tells us to "do this." "This is the cup of my blood...shed for you and for all."[28] A God whose heartbeat, pulsating with tenderness for the whole of humanity, is captured forever in the Eucharist.

A Eucharistic Fusion of Cultures

In the Plaza del Salvador, we were all part of a colorful, cultural mosaic. We were a multilingual throng. Yet, in our diversity, we were by no means a cacophony of discordant notes but rather a hymn to divine creativity. We were humanity "gathered in and bonded by the same Spirit"[29]—different peoples reflecting a collective image and likeness of God, who is community.

Christ in the Eucharist, like the Christ of the Gospel, is the grain of wheat, the seed, sown in the furrow of one culture in order to put down roots and to ripen in every culture—to become the Bread of Life for all of them. "Do this in memory of me"..."*Hagan*

esto en conmemoración mía"…*"Fanyeni hivi kwa kunikumbuka."*[30]
Each culture lends to the eucharistic celebration its spoken language and its body language, its music and its art: the Basque *aur-
resku* danced to reverence the consecration, the rhythmic singing of
the Indian *bhajans*, the haunting features of the suffering African
Christ in churches and chapels in the Congo. And each culture
finds in the Eucharist its ultimate meaning and has its own horizon
broadened in the context of the eucharistic vision of humanity.[31]

Encoded in the Eucharist is the vision of Isaiah, who saw
many peoples converging, after traveling each on its own path to
the holy mountain. Also encoded is the vision of the philosopher:
"Our humanity, not our cultural particularities, constitutes our
fundamental identity."[32] Globalization speaks to that common
humanity and to the common basic needs, hopes, and yearnings
that are generated by it. Globalization also speaks to the relations
of interdependence and reciprocity that flow from it and to the
concept of the common good of all humankind that underpins it.
This world vision involves an awareness of our planet as a single
capacious space, a space that, in the Eucharist, is large enough for
all of us, where the peoples dispersed across our one world are able
to join a global dialogue—on a level playing field and from wherever they are—each making their own contribution and being
enriched by all other cultures, each having their own horizon
broadened. Humanity's song is *not* one played by a single flute or
violin but one played by an orchestra with the combined chords of
all the peoples of the world.

Such a vision is in harmony with the worldview shared by
many native peoples in the traditional wisdom underlying their
cultures and in which a eucharistic imagination would perceive
seeds of the Eucharist. For example, the Akan people of Ghana have
a proverb: *Honam mu nni nhanoa*—"Humanity has no boundary"
—which recognizes all human beings, irrespective of their racial,
cultural, or ethnic background, as brothers and sisters. The social

system of their cultural heritage is based on interdependence and communal ownership.

Also, the *ayllu*, typical of the Aymara and Quechua cultures of Bolivia and Peru, is particularly fascinating. Essentially a peasant social structure to facilitate working the land collectively and in a spirit of solidarity, the *ayllu* is imbued with Andean basic principles in which a eucharistic imagination might perceive eucharistic "seeds." It is essentially a way of being, based on gift and reciprocity: members of the *ayllu* give and receive—and receiving entails a commitment to make return. It is characterized by both cooperation and complementarity. Cooperation takes two forms: *ayni*, which involves the exchange of work for work, and *minga*, when many hands are needed, and work is done collectively in return for food, drink, and a communal celebration. Complementarity in the *ayllu* is about interdependence between the individual and the collective, the community. Both are important. Both need each other. The *ayllu* also involves the cosmic dimension of an inherent connectedness between man and woman and *Pachamama*, or "Mother Earth"[33] in a relationship of solidarity, fellowship, and love. Finally, celebration, fiesta, song, and dance are essential to the life of the *ayllu*.

Two other "anonymous" eucharistic communities are the tribals in India, such as the Sikhs. The tribal people, despite living in the richest state in the subcontinent, Jharkhand, are among the poorest groups in India, sustained only by their traditional values of solidarity and communal property. For example, Sikhism breaks down caste and religious barriers to celebrate the unity and oneness of people. Their inclusive meal fellowships, *gurundwaras*, are always open to all visitors, whatever their religion, caste, or wealth.

Also encoded in the eucharistic community is the ontological unity of humankind redeemed as a new creation in Christ—God's dream for humanity. The eucharistic community makes present the whole Church and the whole of humanity, in prayer and thought, in caring and sharing. In anticipation, the eucharistic community stretches out through time and space, bringing together and making present indigenous and modern cultures, the developed and the developing countries, east and west, south and north until, in the words of Rabindranath Tagore, they meet "in amity, peace, and mutual understanding and this will lead to holy wedlock before the common altar of humanity."[34]

Exclusion as a Result of Economic Globalization

The Eucharist provides a commentary on the twin processes of globalization and marginalization. In particular, it critiques the policies and practices of exclusion that characterize economic globalization. Above all, it challenges the unfairness of international trade practices that govern access to world markets. It is a statement about tariff- and quota-free access to rich markets—markets closed to agricultural and other products from the poorest countries by export subsidies, trade-distorting domestic support for farmers, and tariffs on farm products. It is a protest against the "disproportionate political clout"[35] of already well-off farmers in the West—in the United States, the European Union, and Japan—cosseted by generous government support at home and high barriers to imports, which make it difficult, if not impossible, for exporters in poorer countries, like those in Africa, to compete. The "grotesquely selfish agricultural subsidies that American and European farmers receive"[36] exclude small farmers in developing countries, with little or no trade-related infrastructure, from access to world markets. These factors seriously undermine the competitiveness of their goods in the face of large mechanized farms in industrial countries that have benefited from years of government subsidies.

Examples abound of "free trade" measures that are draining African economies and harming local farmers. In Ghana, where the standard dinner fare in urban areas is rice and chicken, the poultry farms are now unable to compete with imports of frozen chickens that have flooded Ghana since that nation agreed in the late 1900s to allow economic liberalization. Ghana—largely dependent on international lenders—lowered tariffs and cut agricultural subsidies as a condition of receiving debt relief. But liberalization, rather than stimulating the Ghanaian economy and boosting employment, has resulted in a third of the workforce in the poultry industry being laid off during the last two years and the poultry farms no longer producing broilers, only eggs! At the same time, the workers on rice farms report that they cannot compete with rice at its subsidized price of 30¢ per-pound that is imported from Asia and America,[37] while Ghanaians can pay more than $3 a pound for locally grown rice.[38]

Complaints are not limited to a single agricultural commodity, nor to a single country. Ten million farmers in West African countries like Burkina Faso and Mali suffer because of United States subsidies, despite producing cotton at one third of the United States price; the same is true of sugarcane farmers in South African countries like Swaziland and Malawi. At the same time, subsidized fishing boats from the European Union catch more fish off the African shore than local vessels, while African fish exports to the European Union are limited. At the same time fishery subsidies also contribute to the depletion of global fish stocks.

The same inequitable rules apply to industrial goods. The proliferation of bilateral and regional trade agreements can have serious disadvantages for developing countries, which must often accept unwelcome conditions as the price for striking a deal with much more powerful trading partners.

The solution is contained in the Eucharist, translated into economic inclusion. "Most countries, given the chance, would prefer to trade themselves out of poverty rather than live on handouts."[39] Their choice would be to have the opportunity to compete on a more-even footing in world markets, to be given access. "If Africa increases its proportion of world trade by 2%," we are told, "it would bring in $150 B. in extra revenue. That's four times the debt relief offered by the G8."[40]

The Eucharist also critiques the exclusion and marginalization inherent in the structures of the now "old fashioned international institutions"[41] created at the end of the Second World War: the United Nations, the World Bank, and the International Monetary Fund. As with the UN, the constitutions of the IMF and the World Bank should lead to questions about how representative those organizations really are of their members, in particular, their repeated failure to alter the composition of their boards and voting structures to give the fast-growing developing nations a far bigger role around the "table" of the World Bank and the IMF. At present, the voices of the developing nations are barely heard in the decision-making bodies of those international institutions, in what would appear to be a colonial legacy.[42]

The composition of the Security Council, the central organ of the United Nations Organization, and council's decision-making processes also reflect the geopolitical reality of sixty years ago. In 1945, many of the present member countries of the UN did not yet exist: they were still colonies of Western powers. In particular, the selection process for a new secretary-general[43] consists of regional preemption, a lack of transparency, and, finally, the domination of the five veto-wielding permanent members of the Security Council, victors of a war fought and won in the last century. It is an appointment process which, effectively, excludes the UN's membership as a whole.

The world has moved on since the UN, IMF, and the World Bank were created. The post-1945 system of international institutions was built for a world of sheltered economies and just fifty states, *not* for a world of two hundred states and open globalization. The Eucharist points the way to modernization and reform through inclusion.

Perhaps more subtle is the infiltration by economic globalization of the world of sport. A case in point is the Winter Olympics, which, unlike the Summer Olympics, a truly international sporting occasion, could be called the "North American–European Games," characterized by "elitism, exclusion and the triumph of the world's sporting 'haves' over its 'have-nots.'"[44] Inevitably, the nations wealthy enough to host a Winter Olympics tend to be those who win the most medals.

But the Eucharist also fosters the "emerging global consensus on poverty."[45] It nurtures a global spirituality centered on the whole human family, God's children, gathered from "age to age" around God's table. The Eucharist is meant to be a global reality, the sacramental expression of the universal salvific will of a God who wants all people to be saved, who "secures justice for the oppressed, gives food to the hungry"[46] and whose compassion caresses the whole world: "Since there will never cease to be some in need on the earth, I therefore command you, 'Open your hand to the poor and needy neighbor in your land.'"[47]

A deeper appreciation of the power of the Eucharist to collapse the barriers separating the rich and the poor by gathering believers around the altar as a eucharistic community that realizes the global *catholica* in one place, at one moment—be it the Plaza del Salvador, St. Peter's Square in Rome, or the tiny chapel in a shanty town in Chile—will energize our efforts to address world poverty. And a broader understanding of the identity of the eucharistic community, with its eschatological horizons that point to the future, and with its relational wholeness that grounds us in the present as it stretches out to encircle and embrace the globe with its political, cultural, social, economic, and environmental vistas, will prevent us from running the risk of aiding and abetting the growing separation between rich and poor. Otherwise, we will stand indicted as were the Christians in Corinth before us and others more recently:

> How is it possible that in countries where the majority are Catholics, many pious people who go to Church often, receive Holy Communion every day and talk about Christ and adore Him, [also] lead lives that are indifferent in the face of injustice and inequality and, even worse, contribute with their political and economic opinions to maintaining that injustice and inequality indefinitely.[48]

The identity of the eucharistic community is today as it has always been, a paradigm of that "new fellowship in which all are equal and there is no discrimination. It is a goal celebrated ritually in the Eucharist but to be progressively achieved at the social level…a new community of freedom and fellowship, love and justice, which is the new people of the Reign of God to which God calls *all* peoples.…"[49]

The Lord Who Is with Us

God's call is encoded in the introductory words of the eucharistic text: "The Lord be with you." For the Lord of the Eucharist is not a tribal god but the inclusive God of scripture:[50] the God of all, the God of Abraham and Isaac, of Ishmael and Jesus Christ, of the secular multiethnic India and Islamic Pakistan, of each continent and island, and of global religious pluralism, of skeptics and atheists side by side with the devout, of secular socialist feminists and fundamentalist Christians, of the political left and the Christian right. The Lord of the Eucharist is the home of all who search from without and from within.

THE EUCHARIST AND SOCIAL JUSTICE

The Eucharist reconfigures our understanding of both God and God's people. For God is not exhausted by a single revelation. God is infinitely bigger, beyond what any of us can ever think, imagine, or dream. God has many names. The myriad perceptions of God and varying religious sensitivities of peoples are merely a reflection of the tremendous creativity and richness of a God who is perceived and adored by so many different peoples in differing ways, none of which can capture the vastness and otherness of God.

Our global village—which has become a marketplace for the wealthy, a world banquet from which great majorities are excluded and marginalized by poverty—can become a great temple where all peoples will gather to worship freely, a vast choir of melodious human voices, each with its own language, cult, or religion, a great table where the poor can share the meal of life with the rest of the world.

Chapter Two

"Lord, Have Mercy"

The first time I visited the land that is called holy by two peoples and three faiths was in 2002; it was a land in full *intifada*.[1]

It was just before Christmas, but Bethlehem was under total curfew. The streets were deserted. Not a sound spilled out of the shuttered houses. No one looked out and no one looked in. Everyone, the Palestinians inside and the Israeli soldiers outside, was terrified of being shot. Manger Square was empty and eerily silent. We had been given permission to visit the Basilica of the Nativity but only through the backdoor of the Franciscan Monastery.

There, I knelt on the spot where tradition has it that the Prince of Peace was born, and I cried. I wept for a town paralyzed by fear. I wept for two peoples without peace: one of them desperate for security and the other desperate for justice. I knelt where God's mercy, tenderness, and forgiveness came to "dwell among us," and my heart broke for both the victims and the victimizers, who were once victims too. And I prayed: *Lord, have mercy. Christ, have mercy*. The eucharistic words sprang spontaneously into my heart and mind as a response to the pain and sorrow of a broken world, of an often tearful humanity.

Kyrie Eléison, Christe Eléison: A Cry from the Heart

The *Kyrie eléison*, or, as it is known in English, "Lord, have mercy," was introduced into the Latin liturgy in the fifth century, not as an expression of our need for forgiveness, but rather as a cry for help—petition in the deepest sense—together with an acceptance of and respect for difference in others, equals in our otherness.

Latin was already the preferred language for the liturgy in Rome, when the Greek prayer was introduced into the eucharistic text, reminding the Romans that there were other languages, peoples, and cultures out there; that East could and did meet West in the context of the Eucharist. It's a prayer that reminds us, too, that our twenty-first-century xenophobia, prejudice, and racism have no place in God's family. Sunni, Shia, or Kurd; Serbs or Albanians; Hutus or Tutsis; Anglos or Celts; American, Asian, African, or European: all are cherished by God.

Originally, the prayer *Lord, Have Mercy* had nothing to do with confession of sins.[2] It was not part of the Penitential Rite, as it is today, but rather, a heartfelt supplication for the needs of the world. It was a christological acclamation: a reflection of the life of Christ, echoing New Testament passages where people call on him for help in their distress.

> Bartimaeus, son of Timaeus, a blind beggar, was sitting by the roadside. When he heard that it was Jesus of Nazareth, he began to shout out and say, "Jesus, Son of David, have mercy on me!"[3]

> A Canaanite woman, a foreigner, also approached Jesus:

> "Have mercy on me, Lord, Son of David; my daughter is tormented by a demon."[4]

In the fourth century,[5] the prayer had already been introduced into the liturgical celebration in the context of petitions, asking God for peace for the world, for the salvation and liberation of the oppressed, for the Christian community and its witness. There is an obvious social content to the prayer. Archbishop Oscar Romero said: "The world that the Church must serve is the world of the poor. Persecution of the Church is the result of defending the poor."[6]

According to Nelson Kirst,[7] a classic version of Lord, Have Mercy was prayed as follows:

> *Presider:* In peace, let us pray to the Lord.
> *Congregation*: Lord, have mercy.
> *P:* For the peace that comes from on high and the salvation of the oppressed, let us pray to the Lord.
> *C:* Lord, have mercy.
> *P:* For peace for the whole world, let us pray to the Lord.
> *C:* Lord, have mercy.
> *P:* That we may be set free from hate, anguish and oppression, let us pray to the Lord.
> *C:* Lord, have mercy.

At the beginning of the eucharistic celebration, then, the early community called to mind the world around it, with all its pain, asking God, in a collective groan, to touch that pain, but not in an individual cry for forgiveness of one's own sins, even one's own complicity in the suffering of the world. That came later, when the eucharistic text incorporated the Penitential Rite, while retaining something of its original meaning. Later still, it gave the option of integrating the Lord, Have Mercy into the Penitential Rite.[8]

The Eucharist and the Geopolitical Context

True to its origins, the Eucharist today does not leave the world behind, outside its scope, or untouched by its dynamic. Rather, it is profoundly in touch with reality and offers a commentary on it.

The Eucharist gathers us together today in a geopolitical context largely dominated by conflict, violence, and wars, a fragmented world splitting apart: A world burning with animosities, both national and cultural, with centuries-old hatreds whose roots go deep into the communities and into history, fueling insurgency, sectarian strife, civil war, and genocides. A world with sharpening geopolitical tensions, tensions that are particularly high in the Middle East, where the fault lines—sectarian, ethnic, and political—are under intense tectonic pressures. A world where regional and international powers are fighting out their proxy battles over the balance of power. A world filled with the likes of the bitter tensions between ethnic Albanians and ethnic Serbs in Kosovo; the long and bloody struggle between the Sri Lankan government and Tamil Tigers for a Tamil homeland on the island; the conflict and wars that riddle Africa, fueled by poverty, tribalism, "blood diamonds," and the arms trade.

The "risk list" is long and disturbing: the nightmare of international terrorism, rising religious intolerance in almost every corner of the globe, political assassinations, repressive political systems, nuclear programs that could trigger a military strike from Israel, Pakistan, North Korea, or America—all while the newly named "two-thirds world" of the poor and oppressed waits.

The Eucharist speaks to this context: it speaks of the poor, of justice, and of peace. It asks why the world is not doing more to alleviate poverty and prevent genocide and crimes against humanity. Where today the fault lines of culture and creed divide, the Eucharist convokes and gathers together. The Eucharist speaks the truth, with all its complexities, to power, with its simplistic approach to conflict. It offers an alternative to the drum beat and language of war: *Lord, have mercy.*

The Eucharist: Forgiveness and Reconciliation

As an alternative language to that of war, the Eucharist challenges us to recognize our personal and collective complicity in the pain and suffering of the world, and to identify and name our own interconnectedness with evil. "I try to remember that I am complicit in this world," writes Melissa Tuckey. "Even though I oppose the war, I am part of it; it is not separate from me."[9] The Eucharist today invites us to initiate a conversation about our contribution to the conflict and violence around us, as a reminder, before we move into the eucharistic celebration, that we are "all foreigners, outsiders, all blind, all sinful."[10]

The Eucharist offers an alternative to the syntax of victory and defeat, of occupiers and occupied, of revenge and payment for wrongs committed, of collateral damage and friendly-fire. Instead of grammatical constructions that refer to peace merely as a result of war and the cessation of hostilities, the Eucharist speaks of the acknowledgment of complicity and lament, of forgiveness and reconciliation. It offers "a pedagogy of peace," lasting peace based on justice for all.[11]

The Eucharist is essentially about the acknowledgment of oppression and the giving and receiving of forgiveness. The eucharistic texts open a conversation around pardon that is both private and public, both personal and collective, both individual and institutional:

I confess…that I have sinned through my own fault.

Lord, we have sinned against you...show us your mercy.

The eucharistic texts ease us into a dialogue that is both human and humanizing. The Eucharist opens up the idea and reality of forgiveness, moving out beyond the confines of the temple, the eucharistic assembly, and the purely spiritual into the wide-ranging, historical and existential context of reconciliation.

The eucharistic text—*I confess*—also offers an insight into the complexity of both forgiveness and reconciliation, especially when we move *away* from the ambiguity of the psychological-interpersonal private world of our own personal motivations and actions of sin, as expressed in the words of the Penitential Rite—"I have sinned...in my thoughts and in my words, in what I have done, and in what I have failed to do"—and move *toward* the complexity of the events played out on the national and international stage of our sociopolitical world. The same complexity underlies both violence and peace in our globalized and interconnected world, further complicated by a growing pluralism and rapid change. Forgiveness and, perhaps even more so, reconciliation have many dimensions: theological, philosophical, political, juridical, sociological, and psychological.

The Eucharist: A Pedagogy of Pardon

The Eucharist offers a space and a time for reconciliation as a prerequisite for our relations with God and with one another. It suggests a "pedagogy of pardon." It models a strategy for reconciliation, reflected in the various "truth and reconciliation" or "justice and truth" commissions set up in different countries in the aftermath of years of armed conflict, dictatorships, genocides, and other crimes against humanity: the Shoah (the Holocaust); apartheid in South Africa; genocide in what used to be Yugoslavia, and, more recently, in East Timor and Burma; the thousands of the "disappeared" in Chile and the Argentine; the peace process and negotiations around the decommissioning of arms in Northern Ireland. All these reflect a eucharistic approach to conflict. The Eucharist indicates the conditions necessary for forgiveness: narrative and truth, sorrow and lament, responsibility and reconciliation, all within a cognitive and affective process.

NARRATIVE AND TRUTH: *I CONFESS*

The first step in the eucharistic pedagogy of pardon is to admit that sometimes we "get it wrong," or more simply, "sin." It begins with the simple recognition of the reality of the harm we have caused and the acknowledgment of the truth, as an alternative to the automatic exercise of the judicial right to "innocent until proven guilty" and to the plea-bargain strategy. Confession of guilt in the context of the Eucharist reaches out beyond itself, pointing a way toward forgiveness, justice, and peace. It is about naming "what we have done and what we have failed to do," about taking responsibility for both our actions and our culpable inaction. It is about saying it *out loud* so everyone can hear. It is about confessing together, in dialogue.

The eucharistic pedagogy invites the telling of personal or group stories of harm caused and suffered, in front of witnesses. In the Eucharist, those witnesses are the gathered assembly—"my brothers and sisters"—and the whole court of heaven. In postapartheid South Africa, the witnesses were the victims themselves or their families, their children, and their loved ones. The Truth and Reconciliation Commission hearings, chaired by Archbishop Desmond Tutu, offered to both victims and perpetrators the opportunity of telling each other their stories face-to-face and trying to understand one another. These confrontations were part of a process of building a postapartheid society and a possible way out of a cycle of recriminations about the past.

In 2006, building on the South African reconciliation experience, the BBC documentary *Facing the Truth* enabled soldiers and paramilitaries to face, for the very first time, the families of victims of Northern Ireland's conflict. Desmond Tutu facilitated the encounters, which brokered an unprecedented dialogue between those responsible for violence and those who suffered at the hands of violence in the North of Ireland.

One encounter was that between Clifford Burrage and Mary McLarnon. Mr. Burrage was deeply troubled by the events of 1971, when, as a young British soldier, he had shot and killed Michael McLarnon, Mary's brother. Burrage told her what happened, then, reflecting on that, said, "I didn't expect truth to come out as easily as it did, really to be able to put the facts together, to come to some kind of conclusion that helped Mary." Mary, who was also still caught up in that moment, also explained to Mr. Burrage what it had meant to her family and how it had affected the rest of their lives.

Archbishop Tutu maintains there is a need for a ritual of forgiveness, because victims can become locked into victimhood. It is only when they forgive that they can let go. In forgiveness, both victims and perpetrators can be set free from very painful memories, from resentment and remorse. In the Eucharist is encoded the narrative of acknowledgment that is essential for the reconstruction of the collective memory by means of a public dialogue, a narrative that moves all levels— the affective, the intellectual, and the memory—of each person, both speaker and hearer. The Eucharist models a shared vulnerability that can break the cycle of violence.

SORROW AND LAMENT: *THROUGH MY OWN MOST GRIEVOUS FAULT*

The second step in the eucharistic pedagogy of pardon is the expression of sorrow and remorse, translated into apology rather than remaining in denial. Saying "I'm sorry" is the affective element of the basic attitude that makes forgiveness possible. It enables healing, closure, and the possibility of moving on. In the Eucharist the expression of sorrow enables us to ready ourselves to listen to the Word of God with hearts and minds undulled by past failures.

Eucharistic sorrow is about an aching that is able to lament our own failings and also to weep for our complicity in the social and structural sin of our time. It overcomes an individualistic approach to penitence with a deep sigh of compassion in solidarity with those who suffer because of that sin. It allows us to broaden our horizons and to embrace the implications of our interdependence.

In 1970, on a state visit to Warsaw, German Chancellor Willy Brandt asked pardon of the Polish people for the crimes committed against the Poles by the Nazis in the Second World War, in an act of solidarity with the victims of the Shoah and in the name of Germans both past and present. In a profound but silent gesture of apology, he sank to his knees before the ghetto monument in Warsaw in acknowledgment of the guilt of the nation he then represented— a gesture reminiscent of the deeper meaning of the Penitential Rite in the Eucharist.

The Eucharist creates a space for the expression of sorrow for everyone. It makes room for both the sorrow of the offenders and the sorrow of those who have been offended. In the words of Etty Hillesum: "Give your sorrow all the space and shelter in yourself that is its due, for if everyone bears [their] grief honestly and courageously, the sorrow that now fills the world will abate. But if you do not clear a decent shelter for your sorrow, and instead reserve most of the space inside you for hatred and thoughts of revenge— from which new sorrows will be born for others—then sorrow will never cease in this world and will multiply."[12]

The Eucharist also makes time for lament both for past and for the present. Pope John Paul II in 1979 begged forgiveness because of the condemnation of Galileo, and later, on the eve of the new millennium, asked for forgiveness for other injustices, "deviations from the Gospel" in the "dark pages" of the Church's history perpetrated by the Church during the last millennium.

Very much in the present, September 2006, Pope Benedict XVI expressed regret within only a few days after citing a medieval text in a lecture delivered in Regensburg University, the content of which provoked criticism from Muslim leaders and protests on the "Muslim street" worldwide. "The Holy Father," the Vatican statement read, "sincerely regrets that certain passages of his address could have sounded offensive to the sensitivities of the Muslim faithful."[13]

RESPONSIBILITY AND RECONCILIATION:
FORGIVE US OUR SINS

The eucharistic pedagogy of pardon presents the human person as a relational being with the capacity to create events either of communion or disunion with God and with others. In the Eucharist a person is able to take responsibility and to make reconciliation happen, to forgive and to ask forgiveness. It presents the relational nature of both sinning and of pardoning, lifting them both out of the restricted sphere of the individual and making them vertical by socializing the process. It takes account of the repercussions in the community of both the forgiven and the forgivers. This community dimension of pardon in the Eucharist is a model for sociopolitical experience of pardon and conflict resolution. The goal of the pardon process is reconciliation, a process of justice that forgives, heals, and reconciles.

In the Eucharist, it is the offended who forgives: above all, God who forgives—*Lord, have mercy*—but also those who have suffered and the community, too, forgive. Two very striking, modern examples of a real, eucharistic capacity of the offended to forgive are President Bachelet of Chile and the Amish people in the United States.

Michelle Bachelet's father was murdered and she herself survived imprisonment, torture, and exile under the military dictatorship of the late Augusto Pinochet. In her inaugural speech, on January 15, 2005, she said: "Violence entered my life, destroying everything I held dear. Because I was a victim of hatred, I have consecrated my life to overcoming that hatred, converting it into understanding and tolerance, and, why not say it, into love....One can love justice and be generous at the same time. My government will be a government of unity, the unity of all Chileans."

In October 2006, two very different stories hit the airwaves: first, one of violence and, in response, one of forgiveness. A massacre occurred in Pennsylvania when a milk-truck driver stormed into an Amish one-room school and killed five girls. But the greater story surrounding the tragedy was the community's gentle, heart-stricken insistence on forgiveness, a story of the quiet grace of the Amish people, with their distinctive bonnets and straw hats, who place particular importance on the gospel message of forgiveness. They were also deeply upset for both the killer and his family and extended their condolences and prayers to them in a letter to Pennsylvania newspapers, on October 6, 2006. The Amish forgiveness offers a powerful lesson for all and brings us back to what happens in the Eucharist.

The Eucharist reconfigures our relationships. It is a catalyst for forgiveness and reconciliation, an alternative to anger and violence, an antidote to the fostering of hate and revenge. The alternative that the Eucharist offers is by no means easy. It cannot ignore injustice or deny that "what is wrong is wrong." It often involves a struggle not to give in to anger but rather to love one's enemy. It is about the cross, passion, and pain. A few years ago, in Bethlehem, we met a Palestinian Christian whose agony was how to teach his children not to hate. The Eucharist offers a way.

The social dimension of forgiveness and reconciliation in the Eucharist is very movingly portrayed by a well-known sculpture by Josefina de Vasconcellos. It depicts two people, one male, the other female, both in a kneeling position. Their lower bodies maintain a distance, but their heads and arms are arched toward each other, locked in a tender embrace. The sculpture was originally created in 1977 for the faculty of peace studies at Bradford University, United Kingdom, and was entitled *Reunion*. In 1995, to mark the 50th anniversary of the end of World War II, bronze casts of this sculpture were renamed *Reconciliation* and were placed at strategic sites in the world that commemorate the end of war, violence, and division: in the ruins of Coventry Cathedral in England, Hiroshima Peace Park in Japan, the grounds of Stormont Castle in Belfast, Northern Ireland, and at the Berlin Wall Memorial in Germany.

Both the statue, which is a touching reflection of the eucharistic movement toward reconciliation, and the Eucharist itself constitute a prophetic challenge for all conflict situations and, in particular, the Israeli-Palestinian context that, according to the intuition of Marc Ellis, requires both sides to "embrace revolutionary forgiveness."[14]

The Eucharist and Forgiveness in the Context of Justice and Peace

The third form of the Penitential Rite in the Eucharist links forgiveness and peace: "Lord Jesus, you came to gather the nations into the peace of God's kingdom: Lord, have mercy."

In the eucharistic pedagogy of pardon, the hand of forgiveness reaches out in peace, once the wrongs and injustice are acknowledged. However, the door of peace is reached only through the gate of forgiveness and justice. Once it is open, peace lies inside. Then, in the words of Naim Ateek: "Where peace is, a meal is prepared. It is the feast of reconciliation ready to be celebrated."[15] His words speaks strongly and clearly of the Eucharist.

The same theme is echoed in the prayer that precedes the reception of communion, the feast, in the eucharistic celebration: "Lamb of God, you take away the sins of the world: Grant us peace."

The General Instruction of the Roman Missal broadens the scope of the prayer and the following gesture, the Sign of Peace, to encompass the peace both of the Church and the whole human race, in oneness and wholeness. "Before they share in the same bread, the faithful implore the peace and unity for the Church and for the whole human family and offer some sign of their love for one another."[16] The same sentiments have been expressed by Pope Benedict XVI in the postsynodal document on the Eucharist *Sacramentum Caritatis*:

> By its nature the Eucharist is the sacrament of peace. At Mass this dimension of the eucharistic mystery finds specific expression in the sign of peace. Certainly this sign has great value (cf. John 14:27). In our times, fraught with fear and conflict, this gesture has become particularly eloquent, as the Church has become increasingly conscious of her responsibility to pray insistently for the gift of peace and unity for herself and for the whole human family. Certainly there is an irrepressible desire for peace present in every heart. The Church gives voice to the hope for peace and reconciliation rising up from every man and woman of good will.[17]

Eucharistic peace is essentially a social concept. It is *not* primarily an inward reality in the heart of the believer. It flows out of the sanctuary and the confines of the gathered assembly to embrace the whole of humanity.

In his message for the celebration of the Day of Peace in 1972, Pope Paul VI said: "If you want peace, work for justice."[18] The eucharistic condition for peace is justice—justice tempered by forgiveness and reconciliation. In God, all these come together in indivisible harmony. In the Eucharist they are inseparable.

It is in the dichotomies of human existence that peace is pursued without justice. The Eucharist challenges the credibility of that peace, a peace that is uneasy, often unjust, and never permanent. The Eucharist is a catalyst that adjusts the lens through which we view the world. It invites us to look at the complexities of social and political life through the window of biblical justice with its bias toward the underprivileged and the oppressed. It directs our gaze to look beyond peace to the difficult path that leads to reconciliation, fashioned from the burned-out embers of long-lasting animosity, fear, mistrust, and hate. The Eucharist provides a "constant impulse towards reconciliation,"[19] a reconciliation that is sowed with the seeds of understanding and compassion, of dialogue and a commitment to justice, of forgiveness and true peace.

Conclusion

The history and structure of the texts of the Penitential Rite of the eucharistic celebration reveal that the gathered assembly is called to justice. The community is challenged to identify with all those who, in the villages and streets of Palestine, begged Jesus Christ for mercy, and for all those who, in every corner of the globe, still call on his help in their need. Each one is given space to recognize his or her own fragility, in solidarity with all who suffer.

The Eucharist is also a reminder that sin and wrongdoing are never a merely individual affair and that we are all complicit in the injustice and the violence that scar our world today, that all of us need to forgive and be forgiven. All are offered the opportunity to lament, to understand the hurts we have caused, and to come face-to-face with our need to dominate.

The Eucharist does not shrink from the tragedies of our time; it does not attempt to spiritualize them away. Rather, it offers a pedagogy for conflict resolution and reconciliation between persons and peoples: a process of pardon. "No process of peace can ever begin unless an attitude of sincere forgiveness takes root in human hearts," said Pope John Paul II on the occasion of the XXX World Day of Peace, 1997. "Seek peace along the paths of forgiveness."[20] Pope Benedict XVI underlined the eucharistic nature of that process ten years later: "All who partake of the Eucharist must commit themselves to peacemaking in our world scarred by violence and war, and today in particular, by terrorism, economic corruption and sexual exploitation."[21]

In that context, standing with the victims of violence in all its forms and with hearts and minds attuned to God's justice and compassion, we are enabled to hear the Word of God anew.

Chapter Three

"The Word of the Lord"

I will never forget Easter in La Legua, Chile. The Easter Vigil began around eight o'clock in the evening, in the local square. Everyone brought something—a lump of wood, a branch of a tree, a piece of old furniture—to throw onto the already-blazing Easter fire. Every parish group—basic Christian communities, altar servers, pastoral workers in every ministry—brought a large candle to be kindled from the new fire and then taken into the streets and homes of La Legua, to light up the darkness in every corner and every alleyway of the shanty town with the radiance of the Risen Christ.

By the light of the fire, we gathered around the "table" of the Word to share the story of salvation. We were there to listen to the Word of the Lord, like the disciples on the way to Emmaus, when Jesus, "beginning with Moses and all the prophets...interpreted to them the things about himself in all the scriptures."[1] Slowly, because time was not a factor, and reflectively, because no one was in a hurry, we listened as different parishioners proclaimed, one by one, all seven biblical readings that make up the Old Testament introduction to the celebration of Jesus' salvific death and resurrection; their proclamations were punctuated by the full-throated singing of the psalms, a corporate response to each reading. We heard the accounts that tell the tale of our beginnings, of humanity's relationship with God, of his eternal tenderness, of his justice expressed in mighty deeds, of how he saved his people from slavery and oppression, and of his covenant—his promise to care for them always and forever, despite their infidelity. We heard texts that enshrine the principles underlying the biblical notion of justice. We sang the biblical songs, called psalms, about the just and caring God.

After each reading, as the shadows lengthened and the night drew on, a few of the gathered worshippers spontaneously shared their thoughts and reactions to each text. Some told how God's Word spoke to their own lived faith experience, others explained how it was so very relevant to their daily lives, lived out in poverty and exclusion. They brought the scriptures to life against the backdrop of their struggles and suffering, of their own hopes and their fears, as well as the struggles, suffering, hopes, and fears of others like them. In this Easter eucharistic celebration, they grounded and contemporized the Word of God, written in a different age for a different people, but proclaimed in their own reality and heard as a powerful call for justice. They incarnated the Word of God in La Legua.

The gospel account of the resurrection of Jesus was dramatized by a group of young people. As they ran through the square shouting—"He isn't here! He is risen!"—everything suddenly burst into an explosion of sound and joy—a South American *son et lumière* (a "sound and light show")—that filled and reverberated around the square. Fireworks flashed and boomed. A saxophone led the band in a repetitive rendering of "Hoy, el Señor resucitó,"[2] and we danced and danced around the fire, while a huge group of women toppled an enormous, gaunt wooden cross only to raise it again a few minutes later, bedecked with bright flowers. Not a splinter of the hard, dead wood of the cross was visible under that riot of floral freshness and color. It was as though La Legua and their lives had been transformed too and, like the disciples of Emmaus, my heart "was burning within"[3] me.

Easter in La Legua brought home to me the realization that there are significant readings in the Church's liturgical year that embrace a powerful sense of biblical justice, a sense of justice that resonates in a special way with the poor. I also became aware that during the Liturgy of the Word, God's people are called, like the *pobladores*[4] of La Legua are called, to exercise their priestly role as "hearers and mothers"[5] of scripture, bringing it to birth in the drama of their own here and now.

The call to social justice that we heard so clearly in the Easter Vigil readings in La Legua is not an unusual or isolated event. It does not differ either from the main thrust of the whole of scripture or from the commitment to social justice that characterizes the Eucharist. It happens every time we read or hear the Word of God; it is repeated every time we celebrate the Eucharist.

Justice in Scripture

To appreciate more deeply the significance of the social dimension of those readings we need to look at them against the wider background of the priority given in scripture to concern for the poor and the marginalized and the relationship between justice and worship in the sacred texts.

Scripture is the Word of a just God—the God of the two Testaments[6]—who hears the cry of the poor, sides with them, and pitches his tent among them, becoming poor himself. It is the Word of the Almighty, who is rich in mercy and compassion and who delights in justice. The sacred books are packed, from their very first pages, with concern for the poor and powerless; they are permeated with reminders that God is the One "who executes justice for the orphan and the widow, and who loves the strangers, providing them food and clothing."[7] He is the God of those who are at the bottom, on the outside; of those who are the colonized, occupied, suppressed; and powerless; of those who tried and met failure every time and those who no longer try. It is the Word of a

God who asks his people to share his passion for justice: "To do justice, and to love kindness, and to walk humbly with your God."[8] Jesus of Nazareth incarnated that passion in all that he did and said, in his lifestyle, which presented a different way of choosing how to live; in his opposition to oppressive power; and in his mission to "bring good news to the poor."[9] His prophetic mission was to be continued by his followers in the early Church.

Walter J. Burghardt believes that if our reading of that Word fails to detect its focus on social justice, we have not "understood the Torah, have not sung the Psalms, have not been burned by the prophets, have not perceived the implications of Jesus' message, and must inevitably play fast and loose with St. Paul."[10]

In this context, the biblical readings for the Easter Vigil are directly concerned with social issues, providing both a theological foundation and a strategic program for a commitment to justice and the poor. They constitute a call for justice as they tell the story of our salvation, a story told in pictures and symbols. The story begins in a garden with the story of creation, of how God's maternal and paternal creativity overflowed, gifting us and all people everywhere and forever. The story finishes in a city garden with an empty tomb, filled with the gift of life and the promise of liberation.

THE EASTER VIGIL READINGS

The story of creation, which constitutes the first reading of the Easter Liturgy,[11] is the prologue that introduces the theme of biblical justice that is played out as the whole tale of God's love gradually unfolds. It tells how God flooded the world with generosity and kindness and then created us as a human family, made up of both men and women, sharing a common dignity and bonded by equality, interconnectedness, and mutuality. Thus, the relationship of interdependence that is the basis of social justice came into being. God also made us a "hungry people" and gave us the whole world as our food. Food, then, together with all the resources of creation, is God's gift to the whole human family, for everyone, everywhere—both rich and poor—to enjoy and reverence as sacraments of communion with God.[12] He also made us in his image to mirror his tenderness, goodness, and compassion in our relationships and our actions, to be his representatives[13]— worthy of respect and reverence prior to any identification by race, social status, religion, or sex. God made us as beings who would walk and converse with him in the garden in the cool of the evening. God created us as people made to share his dream of wholeness and integrity.

The story goes on to tell how God's care and blessing reaches out to gather all the nations of the earth[14] into an inclusive and universal community. Abraham's test, recounted in Genesis, enables him to broaden his horizon beyond the "me and mine" to embrace the *whole* of humanity as God does. It allows Abraham, our common ancestor and role model, to let go of personal interests in favor of alternative priorities. The third reading from the Easter Vigil[15] describes how God hears his people's cry, sees their affliction, and sets them free from their oppression in Egypt. Besides gifting them with liberation from unjust social structures, God gifts his people with a new social order. It is a social order characterized by a way of life based on right relationships with God and with others: a "contrast society" that will prevent the reproduction of the oppression and exploitation of others that they themselves had suffered at the hands of Pharaoh: "You shall not deprive a resident alien or an orphan of justice; you shall not take a widow's garment in pledge. Remember that you were a slave in Egypt and the Lord your God redeemed you from there; therefore I command you to do this."[16]

The basis of those relationships was God's covenant, or agreement, with his people: God's promise to care for them and to be there for them always, and *their* promise in turn to listen to God's Word and walk in his ways—all that simply because God is helplessly in love with humankind,[17] despite our contradictions, injustices, and sin. The covenant initiated a discourse about justice. It created a context for our relationships with others, especially with the defenseless and those who suffer. It evoked a commitment to reflect God's compassion: to act justly, to father the fatherless and mother the motherless, to welcome the stranger, to feed the sojourner, and to show hospitality to the "resident alien," because this was the way God had acted toward his people.[18]

The four biblical readings from the prophets that follow in the Easter Vigil[19] all speak to the requirements of that covenant. God promises to continue to pour out his tenderness and love on his people always. He will establish them in justice, "far from oppression"[20] and fear. But they, in their turn, must free others who are oppressed. The implication is that, like God, they are to care, nurture, and bless others, rather than exploit, abuse, and dominate them. Again, in fulfillment of the covenant, God will provide for basic needs: "Everyone who thirsts, come to the waters; and you that have no money, come, buy and eat…without money and without price."[21] Potentially good news for UNICEF's estimate that 20 percent of the world's children alone has no access to safe drinking water! But the covenant promise goes beyond access to resources and offers life itself: a new quality of life. In return, God asks that his covenant people embrace and make their own his thoughts, so diverse from theirs that they change course and walk in his ways, so different from theirs.

To enable this conversion, God has given his people understanding: "She appeared on earth and lived among humankind."[22] She is the way to life and peace. So the people are blessed: "For we know what is pleasing to God."[23] But what pleases God is not always what they think! The call is to walk once more in God's ways. Finally, God promises to give them a new heart, a heart like his: a heart that beats with justice and vibrates with compassion for all those in need. His justice will be shown again by his saving deeds, while his people's commitment must be shown in their daily lives. To a people in exile he says: "I will take you from the nations, and gather you from all countries, and bring you into your own land."[24] Their desolate and barren land will be tilled again and become fertile—a potential for hope for the two million displaced persons in Darfur—for underwriting this promise is the creative, generous, and loving God to whom the land, and with it, the whole earth and the entire universe, belongs. His people are those who having experienced exile will welcome home the displaced and share that land.

The two New Testament readings at the Easter Vigil, and, in particular, the gospel text, are the climax of the Liturgy of the Word, as they are in every eucharistic celebration. They focus on the person of Jesus Christ, the Just One, who fulfils the covenant; Jesus, whose death and resurrection constituted the ultimate "mighty deed" that proclaimed God's justice as never before. Jesus' death was the logical conclusion of a life and mission of solidarity with the little ones of his time, which overturned the criteria of power and denounced the partiality and injustice of both the religious and civil authorities. The death of Jesus empowers in us the same commitment to the poor and the same radicality in putting it into practice. The resurrection of Jesus is God's answer to the criminal injustice of those who crucified him. It announces not only that the power of God overcomes death, but also that God's justice is stronger than our injustice, stronger than man's inhumanity to man. The death and resurrection of Jesus make him present in those who are crucified today in a world where, for so many, everyday existence is a bitter struggle between life or death.

The biblical texts of the Easter Vigil are powerful readings, and challenging too, but even more powerful because they are proclaimed and heard in the context of the eucharistic celebration, which is itself a "project of solidarity for all of humanity."[25] Scripture and the Eucharist together are doubly challenging.

THE RELATIONSHIP BETWEEN WORSHIP
AND JUSTICE IN SCRIPTURE

The inseparable relationship between social justice and the Eucharist has its roots in the scriptural accounts of the dynamic and powerful linkage between justice and worship.

The Old Testament prophets made graphically clear the relationship that exists between worship and justice. For them it was impossible to dissociate the worship of God from the exercise of justice. They issued severe warnings to the people and, in particular, to their leaders about honoring this vital connection. For the prophets it was impossible to render worship to God while ignoring the demands of justice. What is more, God finds the very idea repugnant and repudiates any worship offered by those who are insensitive to the basic needs of the poor and powerless. The prophets pronounced this condemnation graphically and repeatedly, while also revealing the kind of authentic worship that is pleasing to God:

> The Most High is not pleased with the offerings of the
>   ungodly....
> Like the man who kills a son before his father's eyes
> is the person who offers a sacrifice from the property
>   of the poor.[26]

> What to me is the multitude of your sacrifices?
>   says the Lord;
> I have had enough of burnt offerings of rams
> and the fat of fed beasts.[27]

> For I desire steadfast love and not sacrifice,
> the knowledge of God rather than burnt offerings.[28]

Take away from me the noise of your songs;
I will not listen to the melody of your harps.
But let justice roll down like the waters,
and righteousness like an ever-flowing stream.[29]

Is this not the [worship pleasing to me] that I choose:
To loose the bonds of injustice,
to undo the thongs of the yoke,
To let the oppressed go free,
and to break every yoke?...
To share your bread with the hungry,
and to bring the homeless poor into your house;
when you see the naked, to cover them,
and not to hide yourself from your own kin?[30]

In the New Testament, Jesus in both his words and actions echoed the same message as the Old Testament prophets. He warned his disciples to be on their guard against those who "devour widows' houses and for the sake of appearance say long prayers."[31] He made it abundantly clear that love of God and love of our fellow beings go hand in hand. You can't have one without the other.[32] He vehemently denounced the imposition of intolerable burdens or the bestowal of social privileges on the grounds of ritual pretexts,[33] and instead counseled his followers that if they have harmed anyone, to "leave your gift there before the altar and go; first be reconciled to your brother or sister, and then come and offer your gift."[34] Jesus also directed his disciples to observe the humble and complete generosity of the poor widow at the Temple treasury who freely offered her last two coins for the service of the Temple, in contrast to the self-serving lifestyles of some religious leaders and to the appearance of generosity by the rich.[35] He held up, as a model of true worship, this poor and vulnerable woman, who in the struggle to live each day, had developed a spirit of true generosity in response to a God of compassion upon whom she relied totally.

We hear the same message in other New Testament writings, but now in direct reference to the Eucharist. St. Paul reproaches the Christians in Corinth for the socioeconomic inequalities that characterize their celebrations of the Lord's Supper and which contradict the whole meaning of the eucharistic gathering: "When you come together, it is not really to eat the Lord's supper. For when the time comes to eat, each one of you goes ahead with your own supper, and one goes hungry and another becomes drunk."[36] And St. James condemns all inequality and discrimination based on status and wealth and reminds the early Christian communities that "religion that is pure and undefiled before God, the Father, is this: to care for orphans and widows in their distress."[37]

When we gather for the Eucharist around the table of the Word and the table of the Bread, we share the eucharistic bread and wine in the context of the proclamation of God's provision for the hungry: "When you reap your harvest in your field and forget a sheaf in the field, you shall not go back to get it; it shall be left for the alien, the orphan, and the widow."[38] The same applies to the grape and olive harvests: a divine injunction that is totally incompatible with today's reduction of taxes for the rich alongside the elimination of social programs for the poor, and with the global redistribution of wealth upward from the poor to the rich. Do we hear the cry of the poor, encoded in the Word of God that is proclaimed in our eucharistic celebrations and which we reflectively break, share, and eat together at the table of the Word? Do we listen to the Word with a receptive sensitivity that enables us to both hear it and to bring it to birth in our world today?

The birthing of the Word in the here and now involves a dialogue between the biblical text and the human experiences and social context of its hearers. Mothers give birth and, by analogy, we become "mothers" of the Word of God when we incarnate it in our lives. This mothering of the Word of God is based on "the theological perspective that God continually acts in human history in ways that are disclosed primarily in the Bible, but which persist throughout human history."[39] It is also justified by the liturgical intuition that, in the proclamation of scripture during the Eucharist, God speaks now and not in the past.

Hearers and "Mothers" of the Word

The Eucharist needs a living context. It is not a disembodied ritual or a religious act disconnected from reality. It is about *real people*. In particular, the Liturgy of the Word is about the assembled worshipers who hear the Word of God proclaimed both in the context of the Eucharist which "enriches the word itself with new meaning and power"[40] and in the context of their daily lives. Those who gather for the Eucharist are hearers of God's Word, who contemporize the good news, making it audible in their here and now and giving meaning to what it says. In so doing, they exercise an important role of the priesthood of the faithful.

Vatican II in the Constitution on the Sacred Liturgy, *Sacrosanctum Concilium*, stressed the role of the laity as "hearers of the Word": "The treasures of the Bible are to be opened up more lavishly, so that richer fare may be provided for the faithful at the table of God's Word."[41] The Constitution on Divine Revelation, *Dei Verbum*, went further, urging the Christian faithful "to learn by frequent reading of the divine Scriptures the 'excelling knowledge of Jesus Christ'....Therefore they should gladly put themselves in touch with the sacred text itself, whether it be through the liturgy, rich in the divine word, or through devotional reading."[42] And *Gaudium et Spes* stated that the laity have a crucial role in applying the Gospel to contemporary issues and concerns of humankind.[43]

For the Eucharist is also about the whole of humanity. It is about the 30,000 people who die every day from extreme poverty, and the six million children killed each year by hunger and malnutrition.[44] It is about the basic elements that make up our daily lives and about the burning issues that affect the men and women of our time: hunger and survival, work and celebration, war and peace, economics and the use of power. The Christ whom we meet in the Eucharist meets us in and through the concrete structures of historical existence—matter, time, space, language, community, and culture, as well as social, economic, and political relationships. The Eucharist is alive with a vibrant relation to the existence and the struggles of all women and men, everywhere, especially the huge majority who are poor—a majority that is growing larger every year.

> The proportion of people living on less than a dollar a day decreased from 40% to 21% of the global population between 1981 and 2001. Development indicators are clearly improving in countries that have laid good foundations for growth....The progress, however, is uneven across the globe....The absolute number of poor people has risen in Africa, Latin America and the Caribbean, and Europe and Central Asia.[45]

When we go to Mass, we take all those people, the world over, with us in our hearts and our minds. When we arrive, they are there waiting for us, convoked by the sheer power of the Eucharist as it reaches out, "from east to west,"[46] to the whole world; and convoked by the compassion of the Eucharistic Christ who embraces the poor with special tenderness. Hence, the Eucharist integrates the personal experiences of the poor, and all those aspects of their lives that are necessarily affected by liberalization and the underlying premises of the market economy. The food security and means of life of almost one billion human beings are directly affected by the rules imposed by the World Trade Organization. Shot through with a biblical sense of justice, the Eucharist offers an alternative reading of global reality to today's emphasis on *homo œconomicus,* "economic man," motivated solely by self-interest. The Eucharist's alternative is instead read through the eyes of the poor; it is a story about real people, a story with a more human face.

Those who truly hear the Word of God cannot remain unchanged by it. According to St. Irenaeus, "our way of thinking accords with the Eucharist, and the Eucharist, in turn, confirms our way of thinking."[47] In a society that has missed the concept of equality and justice in scripture, and where an economic and political myopia perceives the world as made exclusively of "those who have and those who have more,"[48] listening to scripture read in the context of the Eucharist can refocus our vision of reality and correct our mistaken perceptions. It can "attune our way of thinking" and widen the horizons of our worldview. For God's Word makes present the all-embracing tenderness and compassion of God. While "Christ himself speaks when the Scripture is read in Church,"[49] Christ who is the Word become flesh, is told in human words and phrases. We can learn from him to see as he sees and think as he thinks, to speak his language which provides a paradigm to craft our discourse on social justice, and, above all, to conjugate our actions in a "practical commitment to building a more just and fraternal society."[50]

Listening attentively to the biblical texts proclaimed in the Mass, while living as we do in a society concentrated on power and money and yet consumed by hunger for a world that has meaning, enables us to hear what Rabbi Michael Lerner calls the voice of the "left hand of God," the more maternal voice that "embraces compassion, love, generosity of spirit, kindness, peace, social justice, environmental sanity, and non-violence,"[51] a voice that provokes a different way of thinking about human needs and human rights and that challenges the globalization of selfishness.

Those who hear the Word, under the influence of the Spirit, are also called to caress it into life, to be mothers of the Word. During the Liturgy of the Word, the participation of the eucharistic community is not passive but dynamic. Its role is to go beyond the book to its content, its radical message. But it is not enough only to *hear*. As it listens attentively to the sacred texts, the community can make present the scriptures and their message in this time and place. "Without the assembly of faithful believers," writes David Orr, OSB, "the Word does not take flesh."[52] It is the eucharistic community that gives the Word concrete expression. It gives life to the Word in each celebration, bringing it to birth in the dark emptiness of the inequalities of our own time and place. Christ opened his first public teaching in the synagogue in Nazareth by reading a call to justice from the book of the prophet Isaiah. "Today this scripture," he added, "has been fulfilled in your hearing."[53] The call to every assembly gathered around the table of the liturgy and of the Eucharist is to fulfill God's Word now.

The Word, we are told, "gains new meaning and power" in each celebration,[54] for God's Word and biblical justice are not static or frozen in any era or culture. They develop as they touch new ages, new peoples, and new problems. The priestly role of the faithful is to mother the newness of the Word, making the story of salvation a new event that is happening here and now. The faithful also enrich the Word by their response to it. Their service to the world, to the whole of humanity, is to listen to the heartbeat of God, which pulsates in scripture, and incarnate it in their time and their place. "Worshippers," in the words of Paul Janowiak, "are like bread and wine placed on the Table of God's Word. Without these people, there is no presence."[55]

From Hearing to Commitment

The Word of God, according to the prophet Isaiah, does not return to God without doing its work, without "accomplishing that which I [God] purpose."[56] That Word enriched in the Eucharist with "a new interpretation and a new efficacy"[57] has a surprising power to evangelize and transform the hearer, so much so that hearing the Word reaches out beyond the eucharistic celebration, tumbling out of Sunday into the rest of the week and spilling over into daily life—our thoughts, words, and actions— and into the reality to which we belong. Its radical message is both a mirror to the injustice, racism, exclusion, and culture of death of our own society and, at the same time, a voice that echoes around our world in a shared commitment to the common good.

Its dynamism has the power to provoke both a collective response among those who have listened to scripture and "chewed over" the Gospel together, and also a personal commitment to justice that involves every member of the community. "The Spirit... brings home to each person individually everything that in the proclamation of the Word of God is spoken for the good of the whole assembly,"[58] for it is individuals working in unison who form and shape societies. Social commitments are, first of all, commitments of individuals; for example, Rosa Parks. Great social forces, Robert Kennedy powerfully reminded us, are the mere accumulation of individual actions.

The billions who go to bed hungry every night cannot wait for the rich and powerful to come to their rescue. It's up to ordinary people at the grass roots and individuals in the street to make it happen. In the words of Kofi Annan, then UN Secretary-General, addressing the United Nations General Assembly in September 2005:

Let no one be discouraged by the belief that there is nothing one man or one woman can do against the

---

46

enormous array of the world's ills—against misery and ignorance, injustice and violence....Few will have the greatness to bend history itself; but each one of us can work to change a small portion of events, and in the total of all those acts will be written the history of this generation....

It is from the numberless diverse acts of courage and belief that human history is shaped. Each time a man stands up for an ideal, or acts to improve the lot of others, or strikes out against injustice, he sends a tiny ripple of hope, and crossing each other from a million different centers of energy and daring, those ripples build a current which can sweep down the mightiest walls of oppression and resistance.

It is up to the individual hearers of the Word to work together to heal the world.

Conclusion

In terms of justice, when we listen to the scripture readings at liturgy, what do we hear? *How* do we hear? And how do we respond to the readings? Are we moved by the social imperatives of scripture and the Eucharist to *act*? To exercise our "kingly function" identified in the gospel with feeding the hungry, welcoming the stranger, visiting the prisoner and clothing the naked? Do we hear the invitation to recognize the hidden presence of Christ in others? To initiate a radically new and inclusive style of leadership, of loving care and solidarity that restores justice denied? To allow our words and actions to be determined by the needs of others, especially the needs of the poor? Does the Word of God develop in us an awareness of the justice issues that are staring us in the face locally, nationally, and internationally? Are our options nourished by a biblical sense of social justice?

From the early desert fathers comes this story: "One of the monks called Serapion sold his book of the Gospels and gave the money to those who were hungry, saying: I have sold the book which told me to sell all that I had and give to the poor."[59]

The Eucharist caresses our story, each one's story, a story seen through the eyes of God. Everyone's narrative is retold, written by God in and through the lives of those who listen to the proclamation of the Word and who alone can incarnate that Word in the here and now. But it is only the hearers and mothers of the Word of God, like the *pobladores* of La Legua, who can reimagine the Eucharist *with* the poor and *for* the poor.

Chapter Four

"Fruit of the Earth and Work of Human Hands"

Things in this world of ours are not as they are meant to be. "There are structures of injustice with a life of their own, a global apartheid of rich and poor sustained by those with the power to shape global institutions."[1] The Eucharist—as a "project of solidarity...at the service of the least"[2] and as "a sacrament of protest"[3]—challenges that situation and perhaps nowhere more forcefully than at the Offertory or the Presentation of the Gifts: traditionally gifts of bread and wine.

The Presentation of the Gifts takes place with a simple but very significant gesture.[4] It is also a privileged moment that puts Catholics in touch with the essence of what the Eucharist is and can be. It also resonates with all people everywhere who care; it provides a window on some of the aspects of global trade that contribute to the poor becoming steadily poorer.

The underlying principles and spirituality of the Offertory are both accessible and universal in their outreach, crossing the boundaries of race and religion. They blur the line between sacred and secular, overflowing into reality and bursting into everyday life. They make the whole of our existence truly an offering, a liturgy.[5] They also challenge the creativity of our eucharistic celebrations and the authenticity of our commitment to feed the world.

THE EUCHARIST AND SOCIAL JUSTICE

The symbolic language and uncomplicated text of the offertory are intelligible to all.

> Blessed are you, Lord God of all creation. Through your goodness we have this bread to offer, which earth has given and human hands have made. It will become for us the bread of life.

> Blessed are you, Lord God of all creation. Through your goodness we have this wine to offer, fruit of the vine and work of human hands. It will become our spiritual drink.[6]

The key words of the Offertory—*creation, bread, wine, earth, the work of human hands*—find an echo in every human heart. They have inspired poets and rock stars[7] and motivated the concern of the international community and institutions committed to justice and the defense of human rights. They embrace both the resources of the earth—"of all creation"—and basic human needs. They talk to us of food and drink, hunger and thirst, labor and remuneration; of those who have and those who have not, the rich and the poor. Food, the earth, and work are universal for everyone on our planet, yet millions equate these with hunger and greed, rural poverty and agricultural subsidies, sweat shops and company profits. These everyday dramas are set against the backdrop of the exploitation and destruction of the planet earth.

The eucharistic text is pregnant with meaning and embraces a whole host of issues around poverty that are the subject matter of both the social doctrine of the Catholic Church and a rising tide of protests in civil society. Because the Eucharist is incarnated in our lives and rooted in our soil, they bring the poor and their struggles and the rape of the earth to the center of the eucharistic celebration.

The eucharistic celebration transcends mere liturgical practice. It surpasses our own limited experience. It is always bigger than we think and more than we can imagine. It is about life in *all* of its dimensions. The eucharistic gifts, too, imply much more than merely bread and wine. They speak of the whole of material creation and all of human existence. They thrust the Eucharist into the heart of human reality and the whole of the cosmos. At the same time, they initiate a conversation around the issue of land: those who possess it and the dispossessed, those forced off the land that fed them and crops grown on land owned by others. They open a dialogue about human toil and the slavery that today affects millions of men, women, and, particularly, children.

The Offertory is also the stuff of human dreams and the seeds of hope for the poor of our planet, of bread broken and shared, of wine poured out, all celebrated in the context of gift: an economy of gift rather than an economy of commodity.

The Eucharist: Bread and Wine

Bread and wine each have a story to tell, an "autobiography" to narrate. They are *not* natural products but involve a long production process. Crops sowed and vines planted deep in the womb of Mother Earth are warmed and cherished by the sun and the air; their roots soak up the sap-releasing, life-giving energy of the rain. The ripened grain and grapes are then harvested and processed to become food and drink. The story of the bread and wine, like our own story and that of humanity itself, includes a painful chapter. It is a chapter that tells of oppression and death. The grain must be ground into flour and the dough kneaded to become bread; the grapes must be crushed and trodden underfoot to become wine. In that bread and wine, the death and dying of so many people in our world every day, precisely through a lack of food and drink, is placed on the paten and poured into the chalice.

Woven into the story of bread and the tale of wine is much of our own human story here on this earth. Bread and wine tell us the tale of human labor, a narrative made up of effort and struggle, and of toil, tears, and sweat. This toil and sweat are integrated into the Eucharist and transformed by the action of the Spirit of God to become the bread of life.

Benjamín González Buelta, SJ, tells that tale with a poignant passion that transforms the meaning of the offertory, bringing it alive.

> The bread, white and round, on the altar
> holds the acrid smell
> of the dark earth in which it grew,
> the turning of the mill wheel,
> the gentle caress of the breeze
> that cleaned it,
> traces of the hot coals that
> baked it in the oven.
>
> The bread round and white on the altar
> carries the imprint of human hands
> that sowed it,
> in uncertainty,
> the weariness of those who reaped it.
> It rings with the joy of the harvest,
> and the bitter protest against unjust wages.
> It tenses with the struggle
> and competitiveness of the markets,
> the urgent need of transportation.[8]

The story of bread and wine is a tale of injustice but also of hope and solidarity. In his "Ode to Bread," Pablo Neruda powerfully spells out the social implications of that story of bread for the poor. This bread which belongs to everyone, which is made to be given and shared is too often snatched and hoarded away. In a passionate call to action, Neruda summons all to join the struggle for bread "for all the hungry of the earth."

> Then the whole of life
> Will have the form of bread,
> It will be simple and profound,
> Innumerable and pure.
> All human beings
> Will have the right
> To the earth and life
> And so tomorrow's bread
> Will be bread for each mouth,
> Sacred,
> Consecrated
> Because it will be the product
> Of the longest and hardest
> Human struggle of all.[9]

Similarly, in his "Ode to Wine," Pablo Neruda sees beyond the story of the "wine with purple feet," which is "autumn labored,"[10] to its social dimension. For the Chilean poet, wine of its very nature convokes a crowd: it was born to be gregarious, it is meant to be poured out and shared.

From the Work of Human Hands

The Eucharist is about grapes and grains of wheat but also about hands. The words of the Offertory speak of bread which "human hands have made" and wine which is "the work of human hands." Hence, the story of the eucharistic bread and wine is also a tale with a human face, a story illustrated with the many faces of all those work—men, women, and children. In Africa it is the face of the coffee grower. In West Asia it is the face of a woman assembling electronic circuits for computers. In South Asia it is the face of the young girl sewing shirts for a chain of shops in Europe and the United States. In South America it is the face of the sugarcane farmer worker in San Paolo, Brazil, or that of Maria Alvarez,[11] the pregnant Colombian teenager working in inhumane conditions, stripping thorns from flowers in a rose plantation. All these, and millions more like them, are made present and participate in the Eucharist in and through the Presentation of the Gifts.

The Eucharist we are told, "gives human labor its authentic meaning."[12] It offers all human activity and efforts to God, uniting them to the redemptive work of Christ. Encoded in the Offertory is also a commentary on the world of work and all the burning issues that surround it. It celebrates work that is well paid and the remunerated labor that contributes to the dignity of the human person and fulfils their labor rights. It also denounces exploitation and oppression, in particular, the abusive working conditions of many sweat shops, and the inhuman bondage of modern slavery. (A 2006 report by the International Labor Organization estimates the existence of between 12.3 and 27 million enslaved people, including 8.4 million children, the majority of them in Asia and Latin America, all of them subjected to bonded labor or other forms of slavery.) The Offertory reminds us, too, of the unemployed and unemployable. It focuses our attention on rural poverty since the majority of the truly needy in developing countries live and work on the land. It gathers all these, too, into the eucharistic celebration and presents them to the Lord, asking him to transform them together with their joys and pain, their struggles and dreams.

The story of the eucharistic bread and wine also symbolizes the whole material world and contains the story of all primary natural products: coffee, sugar, cotton. Many of these products are pawns in the economic globalization game, particularly in its agricultural policies which hamper global efforts to reduce poverty. According to a BBC documentary—

> Coffee could almost be the emblem of globalization. Smuggled out of Ethiopia, it spread to the four corners of the world through exploitation, conquest and colonization. European countries grew rich on the sweat and blood of plantation slaves. In fact, the global coffee trade is potentially a story of power, exploitation and deprivation and is today a tale of over-supply, falling prices and Third World poverty.[13]

More recently, the bittersweet story of the sugar trade has taken center stage as the villain of economic history. Even though Europe is an inefficient competitor,[14] it has been the principal exporter of white sugar, with almost 40 percent of the world market. It also takes advantage of export subsidies to annually dump five million tons of surplus sugar on world markets, depressing prices and destroying opportunities for exporters in developing countries. "This is a sugar scandal," according to Jo Leadbeater, "and there is nothing sweet about it!"[15]

The Eucharist, with its refreshing vision of the material world—entrusted to us by God as gift, a gift that belongs to the whole of humanity—is profoundly political in its testimony against the usurpation of the resources of the earth that belong to everyone.

It is implicitly critical of the factors that contribute to nearly a billion people being unable to reach or to afford clean water.[16]

The Eucharist is also about food, and so is also critical of the factors that contribute to hunger, the most extreme form of poverty. The World Food Program informs us that there is enough food to feed the world's population and yet there are 854 million people who go hungry every day. In our world, hungry mothers give birth to malnourished children, and every three seconds one of those children dies of malnutrition or related diseases. But it does not have to be like that.

The Eucharist provides a paradigm of the world as it could be. The Offertory provides a road map, its meaning once again in the words of Benjamín González Buelta, SJ:

> Bread can only be offered
> with open hands
> and fingers wide...
> There is no offertory
> From a clenched fist or a possessive heart;
> The claw of self interest,
> personal or corporate.
>
> It is only the raised arms
> Of the whole community that can offer and break
> Something blessed
> By its work and with its joy:
> Bread without a trade mark,
> Without owners,
> Bread set free.[17]

The Eucharist and the Land

The Offertory initiates a conversation not only around those who work on the land but also around the highly charged issue of the land itself, a conversation about the land rights of the poor and about dispossession.

The original scramble for African land by the colonial powers of Europe has largely given way to the present day landgrab involving mining companies and forestry investors, tourist speculators and agribusiness interests, ruling elites and corrupt leaders, together with illegal settlers of every kind. They are the descendants of those who "add field to field, until there is room for no one but you, and you are left to live alone."[18] In Africa alone, Oxfam reports land invasion stretching from the cocoa groves of Ghana to the highlands of Ethiopia or the pasturelands of Tanzania.

The Australian Catholic Social Justice Council recently recognized that "the land we call ours was taken for us by blood, violence and deceit. Its original inhabitants and traditional owners remain victims of our rapacity."[19] The rights of indigenous peoples to legal ownership, access, and control of their lands are still being denied by those who seek unimpeded access to natural resources. Oil is one resource that threatens the livelihood of the Achuar Indians in Ecuador. "The forest is like a supermarket," said Ruben Shakay, in a BBC interview. "It provides our food, our medicines and our tools. But if oil companies come here…it would destroy the forest."[20] Similarly, companies and commodity traders involved in the soy bean industry are clearing vast tracts of virgin Amazon forest in Brazil. The BBC also carried the story of the Mapuches in southern Argentina, who recently rejected an offer made by the Italian clothing company Benetton, saying they could not accept their own ancestral lands as a gift, since they were theirs by right.[21]

Elsewhere, farmers are being forced off their land and into plantation labor or unemployment—so much so that the Offertory raises the question: The wheat that makes our eucharistic bread and the grapes that ferment into the chalice of Christ's blood—are these grown on marginal land, on land owned by "others"?[22]

The Offertory has the power to convoke and bring together those who possess the land and the dispossessed, the landless in Brazil, China, Africa, and throughout the whole world. It challenges us to bring, in our hearts and minds, and to make present in the eucharistic celebration, those whose countries are occupied by foreign powers, for whatever reason. It calls us to remember those on whose land has been built "security fences" that separate them from their own olive groves, hospitals, schools, and family members.

The Earth: Cosmic Dimension of the Offertory

The text of the Presentation of the Gifts sets the eucharistic celebration against the backdrop of the earth and all created things:

Blessed are you, Lord, God of all creation.[23]

It is a text pregnant with meaning and which plunges us into the Gospel and Jesus' relationship with the Father and the cosmos:

I thank you, Father, Lord of heaven and earth.[24]

It takes us a step further, embracing the cosmic identity of Christ in Johannine and Pauline theology:

All things came into being through him,
And without him not one thing came into being.[25]

In him all things in heaven and on earth were created.[26]

If creation is "in and through Christ," then the Eucharist that he instituted has a cosmic dimension. The Risen Christ brings the whole of creation into every Eucharist that we celebrate with him. All of creation is present in the symbols of bread and wine: the wheat fields and vineyards, the roots and the soil, the sun, rain, air, and the seasons—the "sacrament" of the earth. Neruda's insight, again, helps us to enter more fully into this dimension of the Eucharist:

> Beyond the bread
> I see the land,
> Water,
> Man.
> And thus I taste everything.[27]

The action of bringing the gifts of bread and wine to the altar is also the action of bringing the whole cosmos, all creation, God-given as food and life for the whole of humanity, to be blessed and consecrated. It is the presentation of the earth as a sacred reality. It is also about our relationship with that reality, with all living things on our planet and with the universe itself, a universe of gifts.

The Offertory invites us to widen the eucharistic lens to see, celebrate, and incarnate the cosmic dimension of the Eucharist, which has always been part of our tradition and theology, but which has largely been forgotten. St. Irenaeus speaks of human rootedness in the Eucharist in which are offered the "first fruits of all creation." He goes on to say, "The Lord declares that the wine, which is part of creation, is his own blood...; he declares that the bread, which is also part of creation, is his own body."[28]

We live in a world in ecological crisis, where every minute, land the size of eleven football fields is lost forever from the rainforests of the earth and where 137 species of life are driven into extinction every day.[29] This is a crisis which hits the poor harder than anyone else. Often the oppression of the poor is the *result* of ecological oppression. The system that enslaves the earth and the poor seems to be one and the same. "The very same logic of the prevailing system of accumulation and social organization that leads to the exploitation of workers also leads to the pillaging of whole nations and ultimately to the plundering of nature."[30] In this, the Offertory echoes the cry of the earth and the cry of the poor, fused into a single heartrending groan. Just as their twin agonies— the systematic abuse of the earth and poverty on a global scale—are inseparably linked in reality, in the Eucharist, social justice and ecojustice come together.

This reality was both understood and responded to by Sr. Dorothy Stang, SND, who gave her life to protect both the peasant farmers and the Brazilian rainforest. It is significant, in this context, that just a year earlier, the Nobel Peace Prize committee had awarded the Peace Prize to Wangari Maathi, a Kenyan woman, for planting trees!

The linkage between the Eucharist, in particular the Presentation of the Gifts, and care for the earth was persuasively made during the Bishops' Synod on the Eucharist in Rome in 2005. *The National Catholic Reporter* carried the story of two bishops from the developing world—Guatemala and Peru—who insisted that the Eucharist necessarily implies concern for the integrity of the earth. The statement of Archbishop Pedro Ricardo Barreto Jimeno of Huancayo, Peru, was particularly moving:

> As the "fruit of the earth," the bread and wine represent the creation which is entrusted to us by our Creator. For that reason, the Eucharist has a direct relationship with the life and hope of humanity and must be a constant concern for the church and a sign of Eucharistic authenticity. In the Archdiocese of Huancayo, the air, the ground and the basin of the river

Mantaro are seriously affected by contamination. The Eucharist commits us to working so that the bread and wine be fruit of a "fertile, pure and uncontaminated land."[31]

The Australian Catholic Social Justice Council also links the Eucharist and ecojustice when asking this uncomfortable question about the cost of growing wheat for bread and producing wine for our liturgy:

Production methods have often been harsh on the soil, especially in countries like Australia. Unsustainable crops, and unthinking farming cultures, have left huge clay pans as their legacy. Deforestation has had a terrible effect on levels of salinity. Chemical sprays, fertilizers, and pesticides have been used with abandon. Our rivers are polluted and choked, with their banks collapsing and native fish dying out—Is our bread and wine costing us the very earth itself?[32]

The Eucharist commits us to reducing that cost.

The "work of human hands" mentioned in the eucharistic text refers to work that collaborates with the earth to produce bread and wine, and so makes the Eucharist possible; work that helps us remember that human labor is not just a technological manipulation of our environment but a creative and contemplative engagement with the earth to bring it to its full blossoming and fruitfulness. "The work of human hands" encodes a call to work in solidarity with creation, to evoke the fertilizing energies of the earth. It is a challenge to reverence, nourish, and protect her.

The Eucharist also makes us priests of creation in the school of Teilhard de Chardin, with his cosmic understanding of the liturgy and how God communicates himself in the universal

Christ, who is All in All. Teilhard's offertory in the *Hymn to the Universe* is breathtaking as he places the whole universe on the paten and in the chalice:

> Since once again, Lord...I have neither bread, nor wine, nor altar...I your priest, will make the whole earth my altar and on it will offer you all the labors and sufferings of the world.
>
> Over there, on the horizon, the sun has just touched with light the outermost fringe of the eastern sky. Once again, beneath this moving sheet of fire, the living surface of the earth wakes and trembles, and once again begins its fearful travail. I will place on my paten, O God, the harvest to be won by this renewal of labor. Into my chalice I shall pour all the sap which is to be pressed from the earth's fruits.[33]

The Presentation of the Gifts makes us priests in the great temple of creation, giving God thanks and praise for all *his* gifts. It awakens in us an awareness of the presence of God in the womb of the earth. It makes us responsible not only for the human family but for the survival of the earth itself. The Offertory nurtures in us a deep ecological sensibility and a spirituality of interconnectedness that embraces the wholeness of the cosmos. It imparts a sense of mutual bondedness that encircles the interpersonal, interstate, international, and interplanetary. It initiates a spirituality of the communion of all creation; of the cosmic embrace of a St. Francis of Assisi or a Rabindranath Tagore; of the appreciation of Mother Earth, Gaia, *Pachamama*; and of wonder at her varied and delicate living system. It teaches us to listen to the heartbeat of the whole of creation.

The relationship between the Eucharist and the cosmos commits us to work to protect creation, a creation smudged with enormous "ecological footprints" left by our use of fossil fuels; a creation gravely threatened by global warming, evidenced by the rapidly retreating ice caps. The relationship between the Eucharist and the cosmos challenges us to do what we can to lay the foundations of a richer, cooler, fairer, and safer world.

Conclusion

The list of topics suggested by the Offertory is endless and the ideas are manifold, with the connections myriad and the opportunities for thought mind-boggling. The possibilities for celebration are awesome. In the early Church there was already a close relationship between the Eucharist and the care of the needy. St. Paul speaks often of the collections made at the Offertory for "the poor among the saints at Jerusalem": the orphans, widows, and people in any kind of need.[34] The call is to recapture and nurture that relationship in our own eucharistic celebrations during the Procession and the Presentation of the Gifts. It is an invitation to rediscover the vast social implications that flow from the Offertory and allow the Eucharist to reshape our imagination and energize our engagement with global poverty and social justice. The Eucharist has the power to do this.

The Offertory Rite—with just a few words, a simple gesture, and everyday symbols—unobtrusively gives breathtaking insight into the inexhaustibility of meaning underlying the Eucharist. The Eucharist is bread and wine, food and drink. It is white and red, body and blood. It is life, death, and resurrection. It is gift and giving, sharing and caring. It is human creativity and cosmic interdependence. It is hope and promise for the vast family of humanity and for the earth.

In its richness and simplicity, the Offertory can provide a common language that can be learned and spoken both by institutions and by men and women of goodwill to address the problem of poverty. It lends us a new social, economic, and political vision.

The Offertory is a prophetic statement and a summons for justice: both social justice and ecojustice. It can be an alternative strategy for the transformation of the neoliberal economy of commodity and profit into a eucharistic economy of gift and giving. In an economy of commodity, goods and material things are seen as the objects of ownership in a world of "haves and have mores," even of "have yachts." In a eucharistic economy of gift everything is for others, given to us for everyone. In a rich interweaving of giving, creation gives the grain and the grapes: human work and skill provide the gifts of bread and wine, Jesus' self-giving at the Last Supper and on the cross transforms them into the gift of eternal "food and drink," his Body and Blood. And woven through this whole tapestry of giving is the salvific and liberating gift of God, who "so loved the world" and everything and everyone in it.

Because of its vast scope, the Offertory has the power to convoke all those who care, those of any creed or none, those of every race and nation, liturgists and theologians, poets and social activists. Its message is universal, its challenge is urgent.

First let there be bread, and then freedom.
Freedom with hunger is a flower placed on a corpse.
Where there is bread, there is God.
"Rice is heaven," says the Asian poet;
the earth is a gigantic loaf of bread, ours for the hunger
    of all.
"God becomes bread, work for the poor," says the prophet
    Gandhi.
The Bible is the menu of fraternal bread.
Jesus is the living Bread.
The universe is our table, brothers and sisters.[35]

Chapter Five

Anamnesis: The Eucharist as Counter-Narrative

In his foreword to Jeffrey Sachs's book *The End of Poverty*, rock star Bono writes:

> History will be our judge, but what is written is up to us. Who we are, who we've been, what we want to be remembered for. We can't say our generation couldn't afford to do it. And we can't say our generation didn't have reason to do it. It's up to us. We can choose to shift the responsibility, or, as the professor proposes here, we can choose to shift the paradigm.[1]

The great Eucharistic Prayer, or Anaphora, with its *anamnesis,* or memorial, offers a tectonic shift of paradigm.[2] It provides a counter-narrative: the "other" version of history written from the viewpoint of the "losers" on the world stage, the invisible protagonists and the forgotten victims of history, the poor and the insignificant, the voiceless and those "left behind."

At the Eucharist we gather to remember and to tell the tale of why we gather. The Eucharistic Prayer is about remembering. It can provide the international community with a different way of remembering, of recalling persons, peoples, and events; a remembering that is rooted in solidarity. It is the version of history lived and read through the eyes of God. It is a history written by a God who bursts into our lives, who is alive and active in the course of events, a God who remembers his people.

God's Memory

God remembers. The Bible is packed with references to a God who remembers his people and his covenant with them. The prophet Isaiah roots God's memory in his maternal tenderness:

Can a woman forget her nursing child,
or show no compassion for the child of her womb?
Even these may forget,
Yet I will not forget you.[3]

Zechariah, the father of John the Baptist, also witnesses to the power and effectiveness of God's memory:

"Blessed be the Lord God of Israel,
for he has looked favorably on his
people and redeemed them....
[Thus he] has remembered his holy covenant,
the oath that he swore to our ancestor."[4]

The eucharistic anamnesis reflects God's universal memory, the memory of a God who cares deeply for those abandoned by history, the God of all those who suffer in every age. Bartolomé de Las Casas, the Dominican missionary to the Indies in the sixteenth century, expressed that memory so poignantly when he wrote: "God has a very fresh and living memory of the smallest and most forgotten."[5] In the Eucharistic Prayer we hear the story, we read the narrative, of God's love affair with the little and the least.

Eucharist: A "Different" God

Bartolomé de Las Casas held onto the deeply biblical image of a God who "rejoices in the poor"[6]—a "different" God, the God of Jesus Christ, the God of the eucharistic anamnesis; a God who cares, who "so loved the world,"[7] and who wants "all people to be saved"; a God for whom people are important; a God in solidarity with those in need; a God for whom "the despised of the world come first";[8] a God who erupts into human history giving a human heartbeat to his divine compassion; a God who was so captivated by the crushed and the poor that he became poor and humble himself, and who still loves them passionately and lives in and among them today; a just God who continues to opt for the victims of injustice in their social, historical, and conflictive situation.

Las Casas's intuition was also shaped by his passion for the "living Christ, scourged, buffeted, crucified, and murdered in the 'captive poor' of the Indies 'not once, but thousands of times.'"[9] His was the Christ of the Gospel, who identified himself with the poor, the hungry, the thirsty, the stranger, the naked, the sick, and the imprisoned.[10] It is the same Jesus Christ who continues to suffer today in hurt and broken humanity, in the dispossessed and those deprived of the right to liberty and life in Rwanda and Darfur, in Iraq and Gaza, in Srebrenice and Tiananmen Square, in every time and place. It is Jesus Christ whose image is reflected in all the headline faces of human tragedy that flash on and off our television screens; faces that snatch at the hearts of all those who know that "In the face of every person, especially in those made transparent by their tears and sorrows, we can and should recognize the face of Christ."[11] It is the same Jesus Christ, whose person, life and destiny, and death and resurrection we remember with thanksgiving in the Eucharistic Prayer.

Las Casas's passion for Jesus Christ gave him a new vision, a way of seeing things "as if we were Indians," he said. And if this "different" God is our God too, we also are enabled to reread history from the "other side" and see reality from a different perspective—through the eyes of the poor—and from a heart gifted with the sensitivity that comes from the personal experience and privilege of living and working among the poor, and of being befriended by them, with the insight that "walking that mile in someone else's shoes" can bring. I learned so much more about the oppression of women listening to the stories of the *pobladoras*[12] in a shanty town in Santiago de Chile and walking side-by-side with them, one Good Friday, under the weight of an enormous wooden cross that was heavy with the crushing brutality of their daily lives—more than in my study of international humanitarian law or addressing august gatherings on the rights and role of women in our world.

An attentive weekly or daily exposure to the Eucharistic Prayer can gradually refocus our vision and change our perspective. It can make God's memory and passion the paradigm for our own life, our reflection, and our caring.

The Memory of God's Wonderful Deeds

The anamnesis, in the context of the entire Eucharistic Prayer, is a prayer of thanksgiving for God's wonderful deeds, a psalm of praise and liberation in the biblical tradition:

> Let them thank the Lord for his steadfast love,
> for his wonderful works to humankind.
> For he satisfies the thirsty,
> and the hungry he fills with good things.[13]

It is also a narrative that thrills with awe at the wonderful deeds, the salvific acts, of the different God; deeds that encompass the whole of human history and also stretch out before and beyond it. It makes memory of the beginning, the burst of creativity and love that overflows into the entire cosmos, holding it in tenderness, filling time and space with color and song long before we came to be and existed. Eucharistic Prayer IV weaves the sweep of the whole story of humanity into the tale of the earth: "Father, we acknowledge your greatness: all your actions show your wisdom and love. You formed man in your own likeness and set him over the whole world to serve you, his creator, and to rule over all creatures."[14]

It goes on to tell the story of our relationship with God, of our ambiguity and self-absorption, of our complicity with evil and injustice that brings about brokenness and pain, violence and conflict, suffering and death. The Eucharistic Prayer recalls the living memory of a God who cares and forgives, who hears his people's cry and does not let their brokenness and pain go on forever. It tells of a God who really *does* change death into life and overcome evil with good. It provides a memory-narrative that is totally relevant for the people of our time, particularly the child within us all—for *Star Wars* fans who were held spellbound, hoping against hope that Luke Skywalker would overcome the Dark Lords of Sith and set the galaxy free, or for those enchanted by the young Harry Potter, hoping against hope that he would, in the end, destroy the evil Lord Voldemort, and that love would prove stronger than hate. The core of the eucharistic message is in no way foreign to people gripped by the battle between good and evil, life and death. Even the "redemption" of Darth Vader has a "eucharistic ring" to it.

The Eucharistic Prayer is much more than a narrative of wonderful deeds of old, locked into the past. It is not about nostalgia but about actualization. It is about encountering the God of history in the now of the eucharistic celebration. It is about God's action and our participation. It is a living memory of a living presence, with an intensity that thrusts forward into the future. It is a "dangerously liberating memory"[15] that provides us with new perspectives and the clarity of vision of those who see God[16] in the

THE EUCHARIST AND SOCIAL JUSTICE

events of history and in the happenings of daily life. It is a source of energy, inspiration, and hope. It is a "subversive memory," according to Pedro Casaldaliga, that denounces our own part in the great tragedies that assault the world. It also challenges those who remember to a radical solidarity with the oppressed and commits them to embrace the demands of ecojustice. Such are the ethical implications of the anamnesis.

The Eucharistic Memory-Narrative Centered on Christ

The heart of the Eucharistic Prayer narrates the most incredible of all God's wonderful deeds and the most poignant moment in God's story: the "Christ event," announced by prophets and sung by angels. It makes present the living memory of the whole life and ministry, death and resurrection of Jesus Christ—and much more. It recalls and makes present the incarnation of God's love affair with the insignificant and the oppressed, and tells the story of the ethical, social, political, and religious consequences of God's passion for the poor.

The eucharistic text is stark in its simplicity—"We celebrate the memory of your Son"[17]—but it is also pregnant with history and meaning. For the Eucharist celebrates the memory of a God who empties himself:

> taking the form of a slave,
> being born in human likeness.
> And being found in human form,
> he humbled himself
> and became obedient to the point of death—
> even death on a cross.
> Therefore God also highly exalted him.[18]

The eucharistic anamnesis narrates and makes present God's own memory of his Son, Jesus, the Beloved in whom he delights.[19] His memory is of a human heart beating to the rhythm of divine compassion, of the invisible becoming visible—the "paradox of God beyond time, clothed in our days and years; God beyond space, measured in feet and inches."[20] The Eucharist makes present and shares with us God's memory of the entire "Jesus event"—of his becoming tiny, as small as an embryo, then a baby, a child, and later, becoming small again, the size of a wafer. It is a memory of humanity and the school of life, of eventful everyday things and happenings—lost coins and found lambs, yeast rising in dough and the growth of mustard seeds—that is both the subject and the language of parables, that are icons of God's kingdom.

God's memory is of Jesus of Nazareth, whose origins and lifestyle marked him as poor and humble. Jesus, who made friends with the outcasts and the despised of his society, who ate and drank with those on the margins and those excluded from the table, and who translated God's preference for the widow, the stranger, and the orphan[21] into an option for prostitutes, the Syrophoenician woman, and sinners. The eucharistic text recalls Jesus' ministry: "To the poor he preached the good news of salvation, to prisoners, freedom, and to those in sorrow joy."[22]

Jesus preached the good news of the kingdom with a new infrastructure of relationships with God and each other of justice, peace, and reconciliation. He healed the sick, gave sight to the blind, and made the lame walk. He performed miracles, turned water into wine, and, during his last meal, became accessible in a piece of bread and a glass of wine.

There were sociopolitical overtones to Jesus' life and priorities. His preference in his ministry for the outcasts of society and his critique of the powerful among the contemporary civil and religious authorities caused growing animosity, which eventually led to his death. This preference gives an intensity and energy to the

Eucharist as it makes present the memory of the Jesus of the Gospel and offers an encounter with him, as he goes up to Jerusalem to conflict, death, and resurrection. There Jesus "opened his arms on the cross" and "was given up to death, a death he freely accepted," and then "in rising, restored our life,"[23] pouring out on us his Spirit.

Seen against the memory-narrative of the whole of Jesus' life and ministry as the incarnation of God's preferential option for the poor and for those who suffer injustice, the Eucharist can create a worldview of solidarity and can nurture a critical approach to contemporary sociopolitical situations, to injustice and exploitation. The Eucharist calls for an ethical commitment and pastoral responsibility on behalf of the suffering in our world—a commitment that is both subversive and dangerous. Bruce T. Morrill, SJ, warns us, "The qualities of Eucharistic anamnesis are effectively counter-culture in middle-class, capitalist societies."[24] But are they not similar to the qualities that animate the "secular rituals which nourish ethical commitment, through the experience of community memory and the evocation of cherished symbols of resistance and solidarity,"[25] and that characterize some of the nongovernmental organizations (NGOs) that defend human rights, the poor, and the planet today? The Eucharist could be a meeting point.

Martyrs of Memory

The Eucharistic Prayer, which puts us in vital contact with the person and mission of Christ, also makes memory the living testimony of those passionate men and women of every age who have followed Jesus Christ and have shared his destiny to the point of mingling their blood with his through the suffering and violent death that we call martyrdom. The memories of the martyrs are integrated into his; their stories are interwoven into the fabric of

Christ's life and death, into the conflictive political and religious context of their lives and his. Persecution—today, as always, is political in nature, especially in situations of social injustice and the violation of human rights. Innumerable Christians and non-Christians have responded to these violations by demanding a more just world, giving their lives and their deaths in defense of humanity and the liberation of the poor. The Eucharistic Prayer recalls the uncomfortable memory of all those who have resisted, those who have made their own God's option for the poor, with all its consequences.

Although the word *martyr* is commonly attributed to the Greek for "witness," the Greek, as well as many other languages, derive *martyr* from the ancient Sanskrit root word *smarati*, which means "he (or she) remembers." Martyrs *witness* to the life of Jesus. They witness by publicly *remembering*, not just his life, but his very mission of bringing justice to all, especially the poor. Some theologians say that martyrs also witness to or "remember" the future,[26] God's future. They continue now and tomorrow to witness, to remember, Christ giving his life and shedding his blood for the poor, in the certain knowledge that "the grain of wheat that falls into the earth and dies...bears much fruit";[27] a memory in which the future is encoded and which gives meaning to their own self-giving, a memory that makes it worthwhile.

The chronicle of bloodshed— becomes interminable, and the number of people martyred increases year by year. The numbers reflect women and men, young and old, *indígenas* and foreigners, *campesinos*,[28] and landowners, workers and students, mothers and fathers, teachers and lawyers, activists and artists, the ordained and the unordained, deacons and bishops. The numbers are global in outreach, embracing every continent. Some martyrs are well known: the Jesuits at the University of Central America, and the four American religious women killed in El Salvador, Bishop Juan Gerardi of Guatemala, the Canossian Sisters in East Timor, the

French monks in Algeria, the Marist Brothers in Zaire, and Dorothy Stang in Brazil. They voluntarily and consciously took upon themselves the way of martyrdom, their blood fertilizing the Church and the entire world. But there are also all the thousands of anonymous men and women—most of them poor—who have died innocently, victims of someone else's violence, whether domestic, public, or state-sponsored: the marginalized, the humiliated and offended, the battered and exploited. These martyrs die daily, but their deaths go uncounted, like the civilian casualties in Iraq. In them Christ continues "to suffer in humanity."[29]

The Eucharistic Prayer gives visibility to that unseen crowd of witnesses. It makes their invisibility visible through the memory of Christ, providing names and faces as followers of Christ. Pope John Paul II reminded us in *Tertio Millennio Adveniente* that "at the end of the second millennium, *the Church has once again become a Church of martyrs....In our own century the martyrs have returned*, many of them nameless, '*unknown soldiers*,' as it were, *of God's great cause*."[30] St. Thomas defined that cause as that of "justice and truth."[31]

After his last homily, delivered a few moments before he was shot, Archbishop Oscar Romero—possibly looking down the aisle of the little chapel into the face of his executioner, possibly squinting into the telescopic sight of the rifle—began the Offertory with some prophetic words that were about to be fatally fulfilled: "May this immolated Body and this Blood sacrificed for humanity nourish us also so that we, too, may give over our body and our blood to pain and suffering, like Christ, not for himself, but to give concepts of justice and peace to our people."[32]

After Romero's death, the story is told of an elderly peasant woman, who, kneeling at his tomb, "talked with" the late archbishop: "*¿Amorcito*," she murmured, "*por qué te dejaste matar?*" (My dearest, why did you let them kill you?) His answer was whispered in her heart: "*Es que Vos nos querías.*" "It was because you loved us." Happy the martyrs who, like Jesus, love much and give their lives to bring peace, justice, and reconciliation to life. These martyrs are made present in our eucharistic celebrations and in our lives.

The Eucharistic Prayer:
An Antidote for Our Forgetfulness

The memorial-narrative of the Eucharistic Prayer also serves as an antidote for our insensitivity and forgetfulness whenever we act like the hapless Christians in Corinth with their social, racial, cultural, and economic divisions, who were castigated by St. Paul[33] for the myopia that prevented their seeing the presence of Christ in the poor.

The poor, the vulnerable, the elderly. and the intellectually or physically challenged have always been invisible: we like to keep them out of sight, and, presumably, out of mind. They live unseen and go unnoticed, or they are swallowed up in faceless and anonymous statistics that dull our senses, lulling us into idealistic indifference until something happens to bring them to our collective and individual attention. Hurricane Katrina brought the global neglect of the poor closer to home, creating a new subculture of "celebrity poor" in the United States. "All of a sudden the poor have emerged from the shadows of invisibility, lifted onto a temporary pedestal by natural disaster....[They] find themselves in a strange wonderland of recognition."[34]

The Eucharistic Prayer can keep the poor in focus and recapture memory, a vital element in the development of both a critical consciousness and an awareness of both the existence and needs of the poor and of the consequences of injustice. The Eucharistic Prayer also keeps us grounded in God's world, with its light and its shadows, its hopes and its fears. While providing a privileged space in which to thank God for his wonderful deeds, it also offers an opportunity to lament "man's inhumanity to man," so necessary if we are to be empowered to make this world a better place. For, "without lament we ignore the pain and suffering of the world."[35] We tire so quickly of hearing stories about tsunami victims and survivors and of ongoing genocides. We often remain unaffected and unmoved by the harrowing images that flash on and off our TV screens so rapidly we can scarce take them in, much less store them in the memory of our hearts and minds.

The eucharistic memory-narrative also means acknowledging our own responsibility. We quickly and conveniently forget our complicity in the many forms of injustice in the world. Even our prayer can become a "spiritualized" flight from reality, another form of forgetfulness that impedes concern and action on behalf of the suffering worldwide. At times the words of St. James could be addressed to us: "If a brother or a sister is naked and lacks daily food, and one of you says to them, 'Go in peace, keep warm and eat your fill,' and yet you do not supply their bodily needs, what is the good of that?"[36]

Sometimes the enormity of suffering can overwhelm us, leaving us with a sense of helplessness. Here the energy of the eucharistic anamnestic source can empower us to recall the many human tragedies that occur and can enable us to do what we can to alleviate them. The memory embedded in the Eucharistic Prayer impels participation. It changes human consciousness into social consciousness. It is a memory—"a memory of the future," but rooted in the power and the love of God—that can create new dreams, dreams about the ingathering of all peoples around the table of God's family. It creates dreams about justice and a world transformed, dreams like that of Martin Luther King, Jr.: "Go back...knowing that somehow the situation can and will be changed," and, "...in spite of the difficulties and frustrations of the moment, I still have a dream."[37] The Eucharist has the power to "make dreams come true"—both God's dreams and ours. It can fulfill yesterday's hopes for justice today. It can transform yesterday's bread into daily bread, into bread for all *today*, into food for all *tomorrow* and everyday.

Conclusion

The anamnesis is where "liturgical theology and political theology meet and enter into dialogue"[38]—meet in the context of world history, the ambiguity of human actions, and the darkness of evil. In that context, the Eucharistic Prayer is about narrative, memory, and solidarity. As such, it is a paradigm for resistance and protest in a society that has diminished the power of thankfulness and memory, and a society in which freedom, justice, and suffering have no "exchange value"; they offer no lucrative market for consumption in a postmodernity that does not "do" meganarratives. The anamnesis represents the ultimate expression of gratitude and thanksgiving, which both comforts and challenges us.

The anamnesis is about the power of memory, somewhat like the simple oak grove at the Johnson Space Center in Houston, Texas, where present members of NASA keep alive the memory of their colleagues who died on missions, by "continuing to reach for the stars." In the same way, the eucharistic anamnesis is a memory that moves beyond the past into present action, in the living-out of the story in the concrete circumstances of the lives of those who remember. It is about memory, when remembering the past is about shaping the future. It brings the assembly from the once-and-for-all event of Jesus Christ to the present historical moment. It is a living memory of martyrs like Ken Saro-Wiwa, the poet, environmental activist, and leader of the Movement for Survival of the Ogoni People, who was unjustly executed with eight companions for campaigning against the devastation of the Niger Delta and for demanding greater political and ecological accountability of the oil industry in his native Nigeria. It is the refusal to erase memories of prophets, the critical, and the troublesome, and move on—the refusal to forget. It is a memory that keeps alive a vision and a dream of a better society and passes the message on to new generations.

The Eucharistic Prayer is also a call to solidarity that catches us up into the divine reaching out to all people. It is a call to solidarity with the dead, with those who resisted, and with those who gave their lives like Jesus; a call to solidarity with the living, especially the poor, the marginalized, and the suffering; a call to solidarity with all those who care. It is a call to solidarity for *justice*.

The Eucharistic Prayer is a narrative that communicates injustices experienced daily by people the world over and that inspires those formerly untouched by justice issues to become engaged. It tells a story that generates an ethical compulsion to continue that story into the practical spheres of life and society. Above all, it offers an alternative vision of the world, a counter-narrative that prioritizes the poor and takes them as its reference point. If we begin to read events and reality through the eyes of the poor, from their perspective, perhaps the experience of Bartolomé de Las Casas will be ours too. For him the poor proved to be "a voice and witness of a greater Church and a surer God."[39]

Chapter Six

"This Is My Body"

About twenty years ago, Pedro Miguel Lamet, SJ, wrote a novel called *Este es mi Cuerpo*[1] (This Is My Body). It is the powerful story of Carlos Ribera, a brilliant young Spanish priest and theologian working in a Central American country ruled by a military dictatorship. When Delia, one of his pastoral workers, is raped and assassinated by the authorities, Carlos spontaneously recalls the words of consecration that he has repeated every day in every Eucharist, as he cradles Delia's tortured corpse: "This is my Body." He subconsciously identifies her body Delia with the body of the Christ. As the story unfolds, his understanding of the eucharistic words gradually develops and broadens to include the bodies of all the poor *campesinos*, burdened with crosses made from the injustice and lack of solidarity of those who accumulate what is not theirs. His understanding embraces, too, the mystical Body of Christ, the community of believers that has kept the Church alive and true to its founder over the centuries and is still crucified in many parts of the world today.

Later, in Rome, censured by the Vatican for his theology, Carlos, broken and struggling with a crisis around his own identity, is told by his ancient Jesuit mentor that he, too, is the Body of Christ. Finally, Carlos returns to Central America where he is "terminated," with the collusion of Washington. At his funeral, as the celebrating bishop bends over the bread and the wine, his words *This is my Body* seem to take on a special solemnity, as if he meant them to encompass the gathered congregation, all the people that Carlos loved so dearly, and to spread out to embrace the whole South American continent. As Carlos's remains are buried in the tiny village church, the body of the whole cosmos, bathed bloodred by the setting sun, seems to come alive with a joyful and unlimited presence.

Lamet's novel is a moving statement about the Eucharist. It provokes thought, as well as some basic questions: What do the words *This is my Body* really mean? What is the "this"? To what does "my Body" refer? The novel also offers a credible sociopolitical framework within which to reflect on the Eucharist and its linkage with justice and the poor.

"This Is My Body"

The Eucharist is about the death and resurrection of Jesus Christ, the eruption of God's liberating action into the matrix of human history. That is why the Eucharist cannot take place in a quiet, holy sanctuary apart from the world and world events. The context of Christ's death, as of his incarnation, was that of foreign occupation and oppression, together with the domination and injustice of the country's Jewish leaders. Their conspiracy, the complicity of Pontius Pilate, and the collusion of the crowd *all* contributed to the crucifixion. Similarly, the Eucharist is today celebrated against the backdrop of the contemporary culture of violence and death, of suffering, injustice, and all the human tragedies of our time. It is lived against the backdrop of the geopolitical and socioeconomic context of militarism and imperialism that drive before them waves of displaced persons and that fuel unacknowledged genocides. It is lived against the backdrop of increasing protectionism. It is lived against the backdrop of shifting economic might that does nothing to reduce poverty in the world's poorest countries, especially in the

African continent, where hunger still kills more people than AIDS, malaria, war, TB, and polio combined.[2]

The eucharistic words *This is my Body* are repeated daily in a context in which the human body is rapidly becoming an endangered species. A context in which personal physical integrity is held hostage to the arms trade or drug cartels, threatened by discrimination based on race, religion, gender, or sexual orientation; where human bodies are violated by torture, and the trafficking of women,[3] often "auctioned in seating areas of airports,"[4] has gone global. Where even children, the abused victims of cyberporn sites, are bought and sold by pedophile individuals and gangs. Where pharmaceutical companies carry out experimental drug trials on the unsuspecting and unprotected. This is a world in which *corporate* is rapidly becoming synonymous with corruption and self-interest. In this context, the eucharistic words constitute a daily protest.

The Eucharist is about the death and resurrection of Jesus Christ, his Passover from death to life. The eucharistic words "*This is my Body*," followed by the equally powerful words "*This is my Blood*" are a memorial of the death of Jesus: death freely accepted in prophetic solidarity with all the victims of injustice and exploitation. His body, given to all, is broken for the broken of the world, to give them healing and wholeness. His blood, shed for *all*, is poured out in a freeing and life-giving stream, mingling with the blood of those who, like him, have bled and *still* bleed by protesting injustice and the abrogation of human rights so that others might recover their dignity. Jesus, who "opened his arms on the cross,"[5] longed passionately for that moment to show just how very much he loved us.

The eucharistic text recounts that most moving chapter of the story of God's tenderness:

He always loved those who were his own in the world.
When the time came for him to be glorified by you,
his heavenly Father,

he showed the depths of his love.
While they were at supper, he took the bread, said the
    blessing,
broke the bread and gave it to his disciples, saying:

"Take this all of you and eat it:
this is my body which will be given up for you."[6]

In the Eucharist Christ does what he spent his whole life
doing: he gives himself, in a total and radical commitment; in a
kenotic self-emptying that reached its climax on the cross; in an
ultimate act of solidarity, liberation, and reconciliation.

The Eucharist is also, and inseparably so, about Christ's resurrection. The Eucharistic Christ is the Risen Christ. The resurrection lifted Christ's Last Supper, celebrated on "the night that he
was betrayed,"[7] out of its Judeo historical-and-geographical context
and universalized it, transformed it into the Eucharist, to be celebrated at all times and in all places, "from east to west."[8] The
encounter of the disciples on the way to Emmaus with the Risen
Christ was a eucharistic encounter in which he broke open for
them the meaning of his suffering and death, before breaking the
bread of his risen body.[9]

It is Christ's resurrection that gives an even deeper meaning
and broader horizon to his suffering and death on behalf of the last
and the least, of the poor and the oppressed. The resurrection is
God's reply to the injustice that condemned Christ and led, inex-
orably, to his death. The Risen Christ announces that death is *not*
the end. He proclaims the invincible power of love and compassion
to radically alter the course of human history. He proclaims the
victory of life over death and of God's justice over our injustice,
victory over *all* that oppresses and kills the human body and the
human spirit. The Risen Christ puts newness and meaning where
we put destruction, and brings life wherever we generate death

and every form of death: the violent death of war, the slow martyr-dom of the marginalized, the relentless genocide of peoples and eth-nic groups, the inexorable annihilation that is the result of hunger and destitution, the destructive humiliation of torture, and the sys-tematic violation of nature. For Christ rises sacramentally in every eucharistic celebration and brings his gift of new life. In an act that gathers together the past, present, and future; in an act that brings solidarity with all to all the crucified; and in an act that bestows the power of compassion—Christ offers meaning and hope:

Christ has died, Christ is risen, Christ will come again.[10]

THE PRESENCE OF THE BODY OF CHRIST

The Eucharist is sacramentally where Christ's past and future are made present—the Eucharist, between his earthly life and death and his coming in glory. For the Eucharist is also about presence[11]—the presence, not of a long-ago person, but of the Risen Christ. When Christ said, "This is my Body," he meant, "This is me. I am present in this bread."

Christ is present in the bread, in the consecrated host, in every Eucharist. His presence is that of the irresistibly attractive person that he was and is, together with everything he did: his life, passion, death, and resurrection. According to the philosopher Martin Heidegger, *presence* can only be thought of within the dynamic of past and future. In the same way, Christ's eucharistic presence is both memorial *and* eschatological announcement.

It is the resurrection and the action of the Spirit that makes possible Christ's real, alive, and dynamic presence in the Eucharist. The words *This is my Body*, spoken in memory of Jesus and in the power of the Spirit, make Christ present as only the Eucharist can. For the Eucharist is the creative language of God; its text is sacra-mental language. "'The Body of Christ'" is present in the Eucharist as the meaning is present in a word."[12] According to St. Ephrem the Syrian, the Eucharist makes Christ visible and accessible to people today comparable to the way that his incarnation and birth made him physically visible and accessible to the people of his time.

Christ's eucharistic presence is not static, not a *thing*, but rather a dynamic, life-giving, and liberating *presence*. In the Eucharistic Prayer, Jesus the Compassion of God, the Risen Christ, continues his caring presence:

> He was moved by compassion
> for the poor and the powerless,
> for the sick and the sinner;
> he made himself neighbor to the oppressed.
> By his words and actions
> he proclaimed to the world
> that you care for us
> as a father cares for his children.[13]

The Eucharist is also a presence not-yet-but-in-anticipation: "Christ will come again." Encoded in the eucharistic presence of "Christ to come" is the ongoing dynamic of any work for justice and the awareness that the truly just world never coincides with the present moment. In any attempt that we make to seek justice for the excluded and the vulnerable, we grasp that so much more always needs to be done to address the endless injustices occurring on any one day and in any one place. Justice is incalculable, it is always *still to come*. The Eucharist, too, is an event that goes forward in hope.

This eucharistic intersection between future tension and the urgent immediacy of commitment is mirrored in the blueprint of the eight United Nations Millennium Development Goals, which range from halving extreme poverty, to halting the spread of HIV/AIDS, to providing universal primary education—all by the target date of 2015. When launching the goals, the then UN Secretary-General Kofi Annan underlined the gradual process that underpins them: "Success will require sustained action across the entire decade between now and the deadline. It takes time....So we must start now."[14]

You Are the Body of Christ

The Body of Christ is not limited to the presence of the Risen Christ in the bread broken and the wine poured out. St. Augustine broadens our understanding of the bodily eucharistic presence of Christ, saying: "We eat the body of Christ to become the body of Christ."[15] The words *Body of Christ* have a much wider meaning. They are spoken to each one of us: *You are the Body of Christ.*

St. Paul laments the insensitivity of the early Christians in Corinth who missed Christ's "real presence" in one another and particularly in the poor. The Corinthians believed in a disembodied, Eucharistic Jesus, *not* in the Christ who said that he would be present, embodied, in the weakest: those who are hungry or thirsty, strangers or naked, sick or imprisoned.[16] In the Eucharist, the Body of Christ is each one of these—the eight-year-old girl in Liberia forced to trade sex for food, the fourteen-year-old boy killed in Iraq, the victim of "collateral damage." All those with whom Christ identifies himself are his body. They, too, are the "real" presence of Christ. The Christ that St. Paul, "breathing threats and murder," met on his way to Damascus: "I am Jesus, whom you are persecuting."[17]

Patristic texts and the writings of the mystics echo the same theme. In the fourth century, St. John Chrysostom demanded reverence and respect for the Body of Christ in the poor person and even went on to identify the Body of Christ lying on the altar with that of the poor man or woman lying in the gutter.[18] In the fourteenth century, St. Angela of Foligno relates that she went to the local hospital in search of Christ in the suffering and afflicted. She found him there, among the poor and, above all, in a leper whose deformed and rotting hands she washed. The experience, to her, was akin to receiving communion.[19]

I, too, experienced this presence of Christ in a very moving way while I was living and working in Cerro Navia, a shanty town in Santiago, Chile. One afternoon, as I was about to go to the chapel for my hour of eucharistic adoration, an elderly "grandfather"[20] came to the door to ask if someone could take his blood pressure. He came in, and I took his blood pressure. Then we chatted over a cup of tea, Chilean style, and, eventually, he walked away, happy. I made it to adoration, a little late, but as I knelt on the floor, gazing at Christ in the host, he seemed to say to me: "Margaret, that was me!" Never before had the words in Matthew 25 seemed so powerfully real. But that is not the end of the story. The following Sunday at Mass, as I was distributing holy communion, "Grandpa" approached me. I looked at him and said, "The Body of Christ," and his face broke into a smile and…he winked!

THE CORPORATE BODY OF CHRIST

But there is so much more! In the very beginning, St. Paul widened the eucharistic lens to encompass a deep meaning of the Body of Christ: "Because there is one bread, we who are many are one body, for we all partake of the one bread."[21] The Eucharist makes real the presence of Christ both in the bread and the wine and in the body of the eucharistic community. Together, we are the Body of Christ. He is us. The words *This is my Body* both personalize the Eucharist and make us one.

This is the meaning of the double epiclesis, the calling down of the Holy Spirit on the bread and wine and on the gathered assembly to transform them both into the Body of Christ.

Father, may this Holy Spirit sanctify these offerings.
Let them become the body and blood of Jesus Christ,
Our Lord.…"

By your Holy Spirit, gather all who share this one bread
     and one cup
into the one body of Christ.[22]

The Eucharist is the "sacrament of body." We participate in
the eucharistic celebration as *embodied* people. We participate in
the corporate life of the Body of Christ as community, as a local
parish and as the universal Church. The Eucharist is a real, social,
historical, and relational reality. It is about participation, communion, and dialogue; about building up of community and creating
real human fellowship. We are the Body of Christ and members of
one another: "For just as the body is one and has many members,
and all the members of the body, though many, are one body, so it
is with Christ."[23]

St. Augustine vividly makes the link between being the Body
of Christ and being the Eucharist: "You are on the table; you are
there in the chalice. You are his body with us, for collectively we
are his body."[24]

Being the collective Body of Christ is about equality and
unity. Racial, cultural, national, economic, ideological, and social
divisions have no place in the body. We are called to be a united
community with a special commitment to those in need; a body
that identifies with the poor and the weak, as Christ did. "If one
member suffers, all suffer together with it; if one member is hon-
ored, all rejoice together with it."[25]

The real challenge is to be what we are: members of the Body
of Christ, responsible for the care of the other members of that
body, especially the weakest members. The communal and bodily
nature of the Eucharist generates solidarity, as well as the Pauline
conviction that the weakest members of the body are "indispensable."[26] They are important. We need them. In fact, we cannot do
without them!

THE EUCHARIST AND SOCIAL JUSTICE

The Eucharist is also the sacrament of humanity, stretching St. Paul's notion of Christ's embodied eucharistic presence in the community to global presence. Just as the whole Body of Christ is present in each fragment of the eucharistic bread, the local community contains the global community. The total Body of Christ includes everyone. The "majority world" of the poor, together with the myriad ethnic and social minorities scattered around the globe, are one with us in Jesus' body, broadened to global horizons. The corporate Body of Christ goes beyond its local embodiment to embrace nations, international communities, and the entire world in the thrust toward the "fullness of Christ."

The Eucharist makes possible Christ's active presence and his love for the poor of the earth and, at the same time, relates that presence to justice issues in our global age. It proposes a different set of relationships with one another based on solidarity rather than self-interest; it proposes an alternative world to the one currently embodied by transnational corporations, Wall Street, the G8, the World Bank, and the International Monetary Fund: an alternative world in which shareholders and consumers with purchasing power throw their weight behind the commitment to alleviate the global poverty of the powerless; an alternative world in which the priorities of affirmative action and social responsibility are constitutive elements of corporate policy and strategies; an alternative world in which the free flow of global capital and geographical flexibility does not dehumanize either the globalizers or the globalized, a global community in which homogenization of wealth and human services also respects and honors local cultures.

The Eucharist can alter consciousness. It can reveal and highlight the new social and economic divisions created by our corporate and "virtual" world, together with the ever-widening gap between the rich and the poor.

Rice is for sharing, bread must be broken and given.
Every bowl, every belly, shall have its fill.
To leave a single bowl unfilled is
To rob history of its meaning;
To grab many a bowl for myself is to empty history of God.[27]

The Eucharist and the sharing of the earth's goods go together. Hence, it provides a paradigm, a hermeneutical key, for globalization, and a model for the construction of a more equitable society.

THE COSMIC BODY OF CHRIST

The goods of the earth are central to the Eucharist. Without the earth there are no grapes or wheat, no bread or wine—no Eucharist, no Body of Christ. If bread and wine, then, which are tiny fragments born of the earth, can be the Body of Christ, his presence, so can the rest of the creation. Thus, the eucharistic imagination invites us to envision the yet-wider, cosmic perspective of the Body of Christ.[28]

Teilhard de Chardin speaks of the Body of Christ in its "fullest extension":[29] "Over every living thing which is to spring up, to grow, to flower, to ripen during this day, say again the words: This is my Body."[30] A contemporary Indian voice echoes a similar intuition: "Jesus' words, 'this is my body for you,' pronounced over a small loaf, affect also the larger loaf, the earth, which is something we are to share with thanksgiving."[31]

Not only the earth but the whole cosmos is destined to become Christ's Body, fully and profoundly, in a cosmic process of transformation. Creation, St. Paul tells us, is groaning, waiting with eager longing for its liberation,[32] and, together with us, is anticipating the time when Christ, "the firstborn of all creation,"[33] will be All in All. Using the term that normally refers to the manner in which the eucharistic bread and wine are changed into Christ's Body and

Blood, Michael Himes tells us that the Eucharist "is the first step in the transubstantiation of all of creation...the destiny of the universe."[34] The eucharistic text also speaks of that liberation:

> Then, in your kingdom,
> freed from the corruption of sin and death,
> we shall sing your glory with every creature.[35]

But the Body of Christ that is being formed is both troubled and mortal. It is being dismembered by over-consumption and over-competition for fossil fuel and resources. "Seas rise, deserts expand, floods and hurricanes become more frequent and more intense."[36] Climate-induced famine, drought, and conflict are threatening the goals for development for billions of the world's poorest people. This troubled earth, too, is part of the Eucharist and can be consecrated to become part of the process of liberation. "And over every death force which waits in readiness to corrode, to wither, to cut down, speak your commanding words....'This is my blood.'"[37]

The cosmic dimension of the Eucharist has the power to generate a deep ecological sensibility, a distinctive ecological vision and commitment to solidarity with the world of nature. It facilitates an awareness of the network of relationships and interdependence that pervade the whole universe, together with a sense of the wholeness and integrity of creation; our relationship with all living things on the planet, and with the universe itself and our communion with the earth.

At the same time a cosmic understanding of the Body of Christ has implications for environmental issues. It critiques environmental degradation and ecological disintegration, addressing the ecological problems of our day:

> To live, we must daily break the body and shed the
> blood of creation. When we do this knowingly, lov-

ingly, skillfully, reverently, it is sacrament. When we do it ignorantly, greedily, clumsily, and destructively, it is desecration. In such a desecration, we condemn ourselves to spiritual, moral loneliness, and [condemn] others to want.[38]

My Body, Given for You
My Blood, Shed for You and for All

The corporality of the Eucharist engages *our* corporality. For we cannot leave our bodies behind even when we, too, become the Body of Christ. Rather, the Eucharist initiates a conversation around reverence for our own body and that of others; around embodiment and the social issues that are associated with it.

The corporeal understanding of human existence, encoded in the Eucharist, speaks to issues of gender and sexuality, to issues of gender justice in a gender-discriminating world. It can foster critical reflection on the feminization of poverty, which underlies one of the United Nations Millennium Development Goals: "To promote gender equality and empower women." For the Eucharist is deeply respectful of our personal embodiment in a society where sexual orientation is grounds for discrimination, despite the myth that all people, whether straight or gay, are born equal and enjoy the same dignity and human rights. In a world where 6,500 Africans die every day as a result of preventable, treatable disease, and a child, with bloated belly and tiny emaciated limbs, dies every three seconds, the Eucharist calls us to build and strengthen bodies in hope, to bring healing and wholeness to human society.

The HIV/AIDS pandemic is a highly complex phenomenon; a tragic interweaving of many social justice issues. It presents our society and the international community with an enormous challenge, a challenge that defines us both as human beings and as eucharistic people, as the Body of Christ. HIV/AIDS involves physical illness and bodily diminishment, but it also exemplifies a global double standard with regard to its treatment and, more importantly, its prevention. In the West, HIV infection is, by and large, treatable with life-extending therapies and antiretroviral drugs, while in poor and middle-income countries it has become a killer, leaving an army of orphans and creating a lost generation.[39] Statistics reveal the feminization of the HIV pandemic. In 2004, 27 percent of new AIDS cases in the United States were women— mainly African American women. In Africa, 60 percent of HIV-positive patients are women, where often violence is a factor in the spread of the infection. The Eucharist is about reality and, as such, invites us to look closely at the social and economic context of the HIV/AIDS pandemic, the human factors that contribute to its incidence. The key underlying factor is poverty, as are unjust disparities in health care, as well as high rates of substance abuse.[40] The infection imposes not only physical limitations, together with HIV related illnesses, but also the "social death" that is the result of prejudice and possible ostracism by family and friends. Social death in translation reads: "You do not belong any longer. You are not 'body'" any more." In the United Kingdom, HIV/AIDS is now cited as a reason for the deportation of illegal immigrants to their home countries, where antiretrovirals are scarce; a measure that would deprive them of treatment they are now receiving that would prolong their lives. The global HIV/AIDS pandemic raises many questions about the human body to which the Eucharist, a shared communal celebration of living bodily beings, can and should speak.

I experienced the Eucharist as an alternative economy of pain and of the body when I accompanied Ivan, a young man dying of AIDS, in Chile. His gaunt, waxen face and sunken eyes spoke of suffering and pain. His premature aging was rapidly draining the little strength he had left, snuffing out the last flicker of life in his tortured body. But as he lay there helpless, he was a vivid icon of Christ on the cross, of the crucified body of Christ. A voice inside me whispered the words: "This is my Body, given for you."

The corporality of the Eucharist, of the body of Christ, also puts us in touch with our fragility as human beings. In a society based on the illusion of invulnerability, which fails to understand vulnerability as a fundamental anthropological condition—*homo vulnerabilis*—the Eucharist is about vulnerability. It "remembers" and makes present the physical vulnerability, passion, and death of Christ. It remembers that Christ accepted the destructive effects of darkness in his corporal body; that he gave his human body and poured out his human blood to repair our fractured world. In Christ's body, death and life met. In a eucharistic movement toward life and transformation, we are enabled to acknowledge the dark side of reality and engage with it.

We are all vulnerable and in many different ways. Today, the description *the vulnerable* seems to be a new buzzword for "the poor." Women and children are described as the *most vulnerable*, particularly in times of armed conflict and humanitarian disasters. Other vulnerable groups include the elderly, people living with disabilities, those with HIV/AIDS, the disenfranchised....Vulnerability is also a key concept in risk analyses with regard to natural catastrophes and research related to climate change.

Our contemporary society, driven by the "superpower syndrome," seeks to eliminate vulnerability, while it undermines humanity. Whereas, the Eucharist suggests that vulnerability is constitutive of being human and offers an ethical critique that calls for protection and subsidiarity, for vulnerable caring. Vulnerability is the receptivity and sensibility of humans to feel pain and be affected by the pain of others. Our shared human condition of vulnerability and interdependence is a source of empathy and a foundation for solidarity. It enables commitment. The experience of pain can be a source of ethical imagination, of how to diminish the pain of others, and of where to discover others' resilience. It eradicates the top-down, paternalistic distinction of the weak and the strong, the poor and the rich, the industrialized nations and the developing nations. The Eucharist invites us to construct a more inclusive society based on our shared humanity, as it reminds us that vulnerability is a human condition that calls for an ethical and political response and is, at the same time, a human resource with the potential to change the condition of the vulnerable.

Conclusion

Just after I began writing this chapter, I went to a doctor in Fairfax, Virginia. What followed was a deeply eucharistic experience that put me in touch with my own body and the Body of Christ as never before. I underwent medical examinations, tests, and, finally, major surgery. In the hospital I became a member of a corporate body of patients, bonded by shared physical limitation and diminishment. I experienced the gift of communion and solidarity of friends and colleagues who visited, called, and wrote. The hospital chaplaincy team brought me the sacramental Body of Christ present in the host—in the bread—daily. As the days passed, I experienced the gradual transformation of my body as it began to heal and slowly (so slowly) regain its strength. All the time my room was packed with gifts of creation, especially the color and fragrance of flowers.

Even more powerful was an experience prior to surgery, while I was waiting for the result of a CAT scan and biopsy. I was on my way to San Diego University in California, where I was to give a lecture on the Eucharist. As we flew west into a setting sun that bathed the whole sky in an unending blaze of orange and red, the horizon seemed to stretch forward into the future, into *my* future. I was thinking about my own particular sunset, wondering if it had already begun, when I experienced myself gathered up into something much bigger than myself, than my body, than my "thing." My own "sunset" faded into the vast expanse before me, which suddenly seemed to be transformed into a vast altar, alive with the presence of God. The whole of creation seemed to be one great consecrated host, a Eucharist celebrated in the "steppes of Asia," in Latin America, in India[41]...everywhere. Or a huge chalice, red and brimming over with Christ's Blood, poured out for "you and for all."[42] I had plenty to share and to talk about with the students in San Diego.

What does "This is my Body" mean? All this, and much, much more.

Chapter Seven

"Do This in Memory of Me"

To "think Eucharist" is to think big. To "speak Eucharist" is to enter into communion with humanity and to dialogue with the whole cosmos. To "*do* Eucharist" is to reach out to every man, woman, and child that ever was and ever will be—to reach out especially to the poor in every time and in every place. *Do* is a eucharistic word, a verb conjugated as an urgent imperative: "*Do* this in memory of me." Unpacking the text discovers a powerhouse of energy. The Eucharist is dynamite. It can and should explode into action, erupting into solidarity and a commitment to social justice.

"Do…"

The Eucharist makes things happen. In and through the Eucharist, the healing tenderness with which the Father, Son, and Spirit caress the whole of humanity is happening now. The death and resurrection of Christ is happening now. The Eucharist is active: it does what it says. It is about change. The Eucharist changes bread and wine, and it changes us. It has a transformative power and, hence, the potential for personal and global transformation. The Eucharist offers a new way of thinking and a new way of loving. Encoded in the Eucharist is a centripetal force that leads us to communion, interdependence, and international engagement; also encoded in the Eucharist is a centrifugal force that launches us to commitment and solidarity. Within the Eucharist is a dynamic strategy to humanize globalization, taking poverty out of the context of economic indicators, statistics, and categories, and giving it a human face. There is an energy in the Eucharist that is liberating, making present, as it does, Jesus Christ, who sets us free: free from personal and national interest, free from greed and the desire for power; free "that we might live no longer for ourselves,"[1] free that we will no longer be satisfied with the status quo, free that we might set *others* free, and with all of us, free that we might change the world.

Making things happen is the test of the authenticity of our eucharistic celebrations. Making justice happen is the measure of their credibility, according to Pope John Paul II. In *Mane Nobiscum Domine*, he adds that the Eucharist commits us to doing something about

> the many forms of poverty which are present in our world...the tragedy of hunger which plagues hundreds of millions of human beings, the disease which afflicts developing countries, the loneliness of the elderly, the hardship faced by the unemployed, the struggle of immigrants. This will be the criterion by which the authenticity of our eucharistic celebrations is judged.[2]

Otherwise, he concluded, we are deluding ourselves. St. Paul is even more incisive. The Eucharist and justice go together. If that doesn't happen, we have not only forgotten the "story" of the Eucharist, we have also betrayed its power, and its stakeholders, the poor, have been defrauded yet again.[3] The Eucharist without justice is untrue to its nature: it is a lie. The Eucharist without justice is sterile. The Eucharist without justice buried its implicit social concerns two thousand years ago. And then everything remains exactly the same, just as the old Chilean refrain says: *Los ricos vuelven a su riqueza, los pobres a su pobreza y los curas a sus misas.* "The rich go back to their riches, the poor to their poverty, and the priests to their Masses."

In our global context, where some things don't change and others do not happen at all, where promises of aid, trade, and debt relief are either stillborn or eventually broken—the Eucharist's call to action is being echoed by the international community.

There are many examples that the rhetoric of decision makers has not changed the reality of the billions of poor people around the globe. The United Nations Millennium Development Goals are falling far short of halving poverty by 2015. After natural and human-caused disasters, donor conferences abound, ambitious statements are issued, guarantees of aid and reconstruction are multiplied, but the large checks seldom appear. At the 2005 G8 meeting in Gleneagles, Scotland, the world's rich governments made expansive promises to double the dollars, sterling, Euros, and yen given to aid Africa, as well as promises to cancel the debt of the poorest countries. One year later, Pratibha Thaker, writing in *The Economist*, predicted: "Expect slow progress from the G8 promises."[4] Jeffrey Sachs makes a similar complaint that the "United States has promised repeatedly to give a larger share of its annual output to help poor countries—specifically 0.7% of GNP [the gross national product]. But year after year America has failed to follow through. The cost of action is a tiny fraction of the costs of inaction."[5]

This is a world where children should not but do die daily from pneumonia and measles. According to a report presented at the World Health Organization meeting in Geneva in May 2006, drug companies are "failing to meet health needs of the world's poorest....[They have] not yet produced the results hoped for, or even expected, for the people of developing countries."[6] The report cites the existing system of patenting and pricing as fundamentally flawed and unable to meet global health needs. Drugs are priced too high, and there is no incentive to research treatments specifically for the developing world, where the need is great but profits are low: too low, obviously, for the pharmaceutical industry, which is widely thought to be the most profitable industry in the world!

Sometimes failure to help is translated into active hindrance. In January 2007, two organizations, Lawyers without Borders and Doctors without Borders, accused the pharmaceutical giant Novartis of trying "to shut down the pharmacy of the developing world," and of using corporate lawsuits against the world's poor.[7]

The ecology lobby cites the same concerns. The International Timber Organization report, *Status of Tropical Forest Management 2005*,[8] speaks of a "collective failure" to understand that rainforests can generate resources and considerable economic value *without being destroyed*. Similarly, former vice president Al Gore's persuasive documentary about global warming, *An Inconvenient Truth*, received skeptical reviews from oil companies, U.S. car manufacturers, and politicians in denial or swayed by corporate interests.

In this global context of irresponsibility, the calls for engagement and accountability are many and loud. They mirror the eucharistic imperative for action.

"Enough words and good intentions," said Kofi Annan, addressing the international community. "Now is the time of action."[9] His message is again urgent in a report outlining actions needed to follow up on the commitment to make the historic Millennium Declaration:

> At this defining moment in history, we must be ambitious. Our action must be as urgent as the need, and on the same scale. We must face immediate threats immediately. We must take advantage of an unprecedented consensus on how to promote global economic and social development, and we must forge a new consensus on how to confront new threats. Only by acting

decisively now can we both confront the pressing security challenges and win a decisive victory in the global battle against poverty by 2015.[10]

Paul Wolfowitz, president of the World Bank, addresses the rich nations with the same urgency when speaking about the promises made at the 2005 G8 meeting:

> Rich countries must now stand by commitments made at Gleneagles and deliver on their promises.... Momentum for action must also be sustained through a comprehensive agreement that lowers trade barriers for exporters, especially farmers in developing countries, paving the way for greater investments and economic growth. For the millions trapped in extreme poverty, the direction we choose will make a difference between a life of deprivation and suffering and a future with hope and opportunity. For too many it will be a difference between life and death.[11]

The Eucharist invites action from both individuals and from the community. The eucharistic imperative to make a difference is addressed to each one and to everyone. The Eucharist is a personal call to each one who cares and who wants to make a difference: to do something, however apparently insignificant, to make the world a better and a more just place.

Former Secretary of State Madeleine Albright was moved to "visit refugees, persons living with HIV/AIDS, families whose breadwinners had had limbs blown off by landmines, people struggling to recover from wounds inflicted by terrorist bombs, widows whose loved ones had been put to death because of their ethnicity, and mothers who lacked means to feed their children."[12] It is all too easy to feel we are powerless to make a difference. But the truth is that we can change the world a little bit each day. Each one of us can be the change we want to see in the world.

However, the eucharistic verb *do* is not a privatized or individualistic call but a collective invitation to work together. It is a call to the eucharistic community, to civil society, to the international community, and to the whole of humanity to embrace the common good. It is a call mirrored in the discourse of the international community.

In *Larger Freedom*, Kofi Annan speaks about the "imperative of collective action." "If we act boldly—and if we act together," he urges, "we can make people everywhere more secure, more prosperous and better able to enjoy their fundamental human rights."[13] And on the European Commission's Web site, *You Control Climate Change*, every single European, in his or her ordinary, everyday actions, is called to cut greenhouse gas emissions and so care for the earth and protect the poor who suffer more from the effects of global warming than anyone else.

Bono, the rock star and social activist, addresses a wider audience, every citizen of the world, telling them: "U2—you too—can change the world." How? Bono makes ten "doable" suggestions that embrace vision, attitude, and action.

- Speak up for the little guys
- Welcome debate
- Dream big
- Have faith
- Don't underestimate evil
- Be forgiving
- Put friendship first
- Stay in touch
- Keep it real
- Fight for justice[14]

"The punch you throw is not your own," says Bono, unpacking his suggestion about speaking for the little guys. "It has the force of a much bigger issue."[15] That much bigger issue is part of the eucharistic conversion implied in "Do this in memory of me" with its demands and its dreams.

"Do This..."

When Jesus said "Do this in memory of me," what was the *this* he had in mind? St. Paul, our earliest witness to the Eucharist, describes it variously as the *Lord's Supper*, the *Breaking of Bread*, and *Communion*. These three images are a key to understanding something of the life, mindset, and spirituality embraced by the eucharistic *this*, together with the underlying theological, social, and economic dimensions it embraces as well.

The Lord's Supper

The Eucharist is a supper, originally celebrated by Jesus at his Last Supper. It is a meal that is meant to be a banquet, a feast. But there can be no meal where there is little or no food or drink. In our world, millions of hungry people beg for their daily bread, over nine million die every year from malnutrition, and 24,500 children die every day from hunger-related causes.[16]

The socioeconomic implications of the Lord's Supper, of the eucharistic *this*, are illustrated in the description of the early Church. It was a potentially subversive community, made up of Jews and non-Jews, freemen and slaves, men and women, and rich and poor, in which:

All who believed lived together and had all things in common....They broke bread at home and ate their food with glad and generous hearts.

There was not a needy person among them, for as many as owned land or houses sold them and brought the proceeds of what was sold. They laid it at the apostles' feet, and it was distributed to each as any had need.[17]

In the same spirit, St. Paul urged the early Christian communities that he had founded in Galatia, Macedonia, and Corinth to make a collection "in aid of the famine stricken church in Jerusalem."[18]

The Eucharist "says," as Jesus himself said to his disciples, "You give them something to eat."[19] A demand of the Eucharist is that every person, every family, every village, every nation should have daily bread or rice or whatever their staple food happens to be. Where there is no bread, no rice today, only yesterday's leftovers from someone else's table, there can be no Eucharist. No one, especially the children of the world, should go to bed hungry and thirsty. The obligation is to feed the hungry, to offer a feast to the starving.

The Eucharist looks forward to a banquet in which the wealthy and the poor will feast together: "In that new world where the fullness of your peace will be revealed, gather together people of every race, language, and way of life to share in the one eternal banquet."[20]

The Eucharist is a meal that evokes the equality of the table-sharing of Jesus' meals in the Gospels: a table with no conditions for participation; a table with no social stratification, no gender distinctions, no form of inequality, no discrimination, and no dualism. This is a table that honors the traditional preparers and servers of family meals: the mothers, wives, sisters, and daughters who have so many mouths to fill each day but who so often cannot do so because of famine, drought, or war; "the women who preside at life's Eucharistic banquet, breaking the bread of their lives to feed the hungry of the world."[21]

THE BREAKING OF BREAD

The Eucharist is not just about bread and wine, but rather, bread *broken* and wine *poured out*, "given for you."[22] Jesus took the bread and broke it, in a prophetic gesture of total self-giving, prefaced by the washing of the feet of his disciples, and later accomplished by the shedding of his own blood. Jesus' voluntary self-giving for others was the priority that characterized the whole of his event-filled life and mission. The Gospels tell us that, from early in the morning, everybody was looking for him,[23] and that his ministry left him "no leisure even to eat."[24] This way of life reached its climax in his death, when "he opened his arms on the cross,"[25] in a final act of self-emptying. Jesus' identity, who he was and what he did, is encoded in the breaking of bread. That is how the disciples on the way to Emmaus recognized him. The Eucharist is where we, too, will find him, as well as in its call to continue his self-giving and service to the poor and underprivileged and to social and personal involvement, each from within our own sociopolitical and economic situation.

Jesus broke the bread and said, "Do this," in the shadow of the cross, in the context of betrayal and injustice, and against the background of apparent failure and powerlessness. Jesus himself experienced suffering and understood pain; he knew the pain of torture, abandonment, and death. He broke bread in a eucharistic logic totally opposed to the "logic" of torture and violence.[26] He broke bread in solidarity with the bruised and the broken, with the suffering and the persecuted. He broke bread in appreciation of those who lament the pain and suffering of the world on the international stage, and who grieve for the broken connections in our society.

There, at the foot of the cross, and in the breaking of the bread, we cannot ignore the tragedies of our time. The Eucharist is a source of energy to recall and listen to stories of survivors and of their pain. It furnishes a basis for social criticism and the evaluation of the structures of society. It is an inspiration to enflesh the Eucharist in daily life, in *our* being bread that is broken and in *our* risking our lives, when necessary, in the face of injustice. It is a call to what Jon Sobrino calls "political sanctity"[27]—an aching solidarity with the suffering and a selfless courage in the face of adversity, in contexts where resisting domination and the eradication of civil liberties can lead to persecution, and where dissent and constructive protest sometimes may mean death.

Jesus also broke the bread so there would be enough to go around for those seated at the table with him. It was something he had done before. In the Gospel we read how Jesus took five loaves, and then blessed and broke them so there would be enough to feed five thousand people.[28] So in his words *Do this*, the eucharistic *this* is also about sharing, making sure that there is enough for everyone. The Eucharist offers an alternative to greed. It advocates giving to the point of excess, a profligate generosity, in stark contrast to a marketplace logic of the maximization of self-interest and the acquisition of material goods and comforts, which characterizes a society based on a bottom line of money and power. The Eucharist critiques the disconnect between what people really need and a supply-and-demand economy, possessiveness, the attitude of "me-first," and the culture of consumerism with its obsessive appropriation and accumulation of things.

We are sent out from the Eucharist to make a difference, to support the *new* bottom line that is emerging from social responsibility to the common good. We are sent out to prioritize sharing—the caring economy which is at the heart of the Eucharist—and to emphasize the urgency of building a new social order based on kindness and generosity. The Eucharist is lived as compassionate loving.

It is a gift received in the giving. A proper response to the Eucharist is the dissemination of gift and giving in the lives of others.

COMMUNION

In communion we eat and drink together the Body and Blood of Christ. We commune with both the divine and the human, as individuals and as community. We enter into communion with God but also into the horizontal communion of all peoples. The Eucharist doesn't "do" individualism. Eucharistic conversion rules out unilateralism. Rather, it fosters unity, togetherness, and cooperation. As Rabbi Michael Lerner said in *The Left Hand of God*, it emphasizes "mutual cooperation, recognition of the spirit of God in every other human being and awareness of our interdependence with others, responsibility to the well-being of the planet, and a powerful sense of awe and wonder at the grandeur of creation."[29]

In our multicultural, multireligious, and multiethnic society, the Eucharist can foster a spirituality of communion and dialogue, developing our capacity to listen and understand, and enabling us to hear and to converse, to give and to receive, and to respect and to reverence the other in equality. It encourages the ability to "be enlarged by the presence of others who think, act, and interpret reality in ways radically different from our own."[30] In this context, ecclesial communion is not so much about conformity, but rather about shared faith in Jesus Christ and creative fidelity in our commitment to the kingdom of God.

Eucharistic communion counters a myopic, ethnocentric, and domineering monologic approach to others with a shared vision of humanity, and with a shared belief in the dignity of difference and the richness of pluralism. It undermines arrogant superiority with an openness and humility that go with putting "on the same mind that was in Christ Jesus," who emptied himself[31] for us. Communion is about complementarity and compromise, about

106

forgiveness and reconciliation. It states, in effect, that cultures don't have to clash, that there do not have to be either winners or losers. That polarization, that social fragmentation—be it religious or political—can be overcome by an acknowledgment of the integrity of those who are different from us and who think differently from us. It can be overcome by an authentic commitment to interreligious dialogue and ecumenism that will disarm fundamentalisms. Communion is about being connected and communicating, being willing to talk, without preconditions.

But communion is not just about minds and hearts, words and attitudes, but also about the "communication of goods" that makes communion visible and tangible; the communication of the real, the material, and the economic. It is about economic sacrifice for the sake of justice. "Specialists in the field," writes Madeleine Albright, in *The Mighty and the Almighty*, "have learned more about how to make effective use of aid dollars by channeling the majority of funds through nongovernmental institutions, emphasizing opportunities for women, stressing low-tech solutions, heeding environmental considerations, and finding ways to let even the poorest participate economically."[32] Communion is about being in love with Christ and in love with the world.

"Do This in Memory of Me"

Two Jewish feasts form the context of the Christian Eucharist. Both set the scene for Jesus' instruction to "do this in memory of me." Passover and the immediately following Feast of Unleavened Bread caress the memory of the birth of freedom, of God's liberating intervention on behalf of his enslaved and oppressed people, and of his caring presence on their journey toward their promised land and liberty. In a Jewish context, *memory* does not signify an action already completed but an action that is taking place. It does not take us back into the past, but brings God's presence and action into the present. Hence, in the same way, a eucharistic memory does not go back to Jesus Christ, but rather it actualizes "the event" that was Jesus in the here and now. It provokes a vital encounter with the person and mission of Jesus.

The words *In memory of me* center the Eucharist on the person of Jesus, bringing not only Jesus' Last Supper but the washing of the feet of his disciples and all the explicit eucharistic memories in the Gospel into the present moment. In the Gospel of John, the washing of the feet is a eucharistic narrative that concludes with Jesus telling his disciples to do what he has just done.[33] Jesus also fed hungry crowds in lonely places. He told the parents of the twelve-year-old girl he had raised from the dead to give her something to eat.[34] He told his disciples that he was the Bread of Life.[35] He continually gave thanks to the Father and blessed him for revealing to the little ones secrets kept hidden from the wise and the learned.[36] In a profoundly eucharistic passage in Matthew's Gospel, Jesus identifies himself with the last and the least, affirming that what is done to them is done to him.[37]

In fact, the whole life of Christ was eucharistic, one enormous eucharistic memory. The Eucharist recalls the whole "Christ event," from his incarnation to his death and resurrection. In the incarnation, "the Word became flesh and lived among us,"[38] through the creative and transforming action of the Spirit, which makes the human divine and the divine human; it is the same Spirit that transforms the bread and wine into the Body and Blood of Christ. In his kenotic incarnation, God made himself tiny, as we have said before, a fetus, a baby, a little child. In the Eucharist, he becomes tiny, too, the size of a wafer. The shape of his humanity is now a small piece of bread. Michelangelo's exquisite *Pietà* depicts the Body of Christ taken down from the cross and cradled tenderly, reverently, placed on the "paten" of Mary's lap in a gesture reminiscent of his eucharistic Body laid on the altar in memory of his human death for all humanity.

In memory of me recalls Jesus' passionate desire to share our lives and to be one of us, to be our kin. In the Eucharist, memory of him embraces all things human, humanity itself, all people, all men, women, and children, with all their hopes and their fears, their work and their play, their joys and their sorrows. Jesus was sowed in the furrow of one culture, one race, and one time yet puts down roots in all of them. The Eucharist also gathers up all human memories of table and celebration, of food and fun, of merriment and mirth, of laughter and of tears.

The eucharistic memory is centered on Jesus. It is celebrated "in memory of him." But it is not just a recollection of his life. It is a living memory, a memory of love; a memory of loving tenderly, of doing justice, and of walking humbly with God.[39] Imbedded in eucharistic memory is a commitment to enter into the strange yet dynamic logic of Christ's love. Christ was a man for God and for others. He was madly in love with humanity—he loved us to death. Christ's love created a new dream for the world, a new song, the song sung by the angels when he was born. The new dream became reality wherever Jesus passed: the blind saw, the lame walked, the lepers were cleansed, the deaf heard, and the good news was preached to the poor.[40] Jesus proposed as a model the good Samaritan, who cared for a wounded stranger and set up a structure for dealing with his future needs.[41] Jesus' critical approach to the contemporary sociopolitical and religious order was directed to the setting up of a new order based on freedom, equality, fellowship, and the common good. The memory of Jesus takes us to a new time and place. It gives us a new memory where the dream can become a historical reality, as it did in Jesus' lifetime. The source of that newness is Eucharist:

> Through him, with him, and in him, in the fellowship
> of the Holy Spirit.[42]

The paradigm is imbedded in the memory of Jesus, a memory that overflows beyond the eucharistic celebration into what we do, and why we do it; into doing what Jesus did and the way he did it.

Conclusion

The Eucharist is essentially dynamic and active, enabling us to "do this," all of it. But "do this in memory of me" refers, above all, to God's action, making the impossible *possible*. It's not about us but about God, about God's tumbling into our lives. We are called just to be there and let it happen. The Eucharist is about God's activity in and through everyone and everything. In God's activity, *all* is gift. The Eucharist invites us to the adventure of gift, of *being* gift, and of *gratuitous* giving to others, especially those in need. For that reason, the Eucharist is a comment on the reduction of aid to the Third World from richer countries in recent years, on trade rules and on debt.

God's Spirit is present and at work in our society in so many surprising ways: in all the bursts of creativity, solidarity, and communion that are pulsating through our weary world; in the broadening awareness of global poverty; and in the opening up of new possibilities for action. God is acting through new leadership in Africa and other poor parts of world where democracies are embarking on new ways to combat corruption and create more transparent governance, which will make effective aid and real economic development possible. God is acting through the leaders of the world's wealthiest nations, the G8, in their ongoing, if stumbling, deliberations, and in the ever-greater public pressure that is being brought to bear on them. God is acting through the many religious leaders and faith communities in their shared humanitarian responses to issues around poverty and injustice. God is acting through the new coalitions that are networking for Darfur, AIDS, peace, the Amazon rain forest, and human rights. God is acting through NGOs, civil society, and the growing demand of share-holders and customers that multinational companies embrace corporate social responsibility; that they do good as well as do well.

Do this is memory of me is about eucharistic conversion—a new lifestyle, mindset, and spirituality.

> *Llamados por la luz de Tu memoria,*
> *marchamos hacia el Reino haciendo Historia*
> *fraterna y subversiva Eucaristía.*

> Called by the light of your memory,
> we journey toward the kingdom, making history,
> fraternal and subversive Eucharist.[43]

The Eucharist is subversive, undermining our selfishness, undermining our often-unknowing complicity with injustice. It is about seeing the world through eucharistic eyes and trying to make a difference wherever we are. It is about making hope strategic for both the rich and the poor. It is about rewriting politics and reimagining justice. But, to do that, we need a wider understanding of the Eucharist and its context, together with a more-acute and more-critical political awareness. My studies in theology, particularly eucharistic theology, and in international relations go together in a challenging dialectic. They both serve as catalysts that continually reshape my experience as a eucharistic woman and a citizen of the world in the twenty-first century.

The inexhaustible richness and potential of the Eucharist is always inviting us to deeper reflection and more authentic celebration. The eucharistic bread is deeply challenging in our throwaway culture, in which so many of our brothers and sisters spend their time and energy in the landfills of the world, looking for yesterday's bread.

"The great challenge today is to convert the sacred bread into real bread....It is risky to celebrate Eucharist. We may have to leave it unfinished, having gone first to give back to the poor what belongs to them."[44]

It is the challenge to convert yesterday's bread into bread today—bread today for everyone.

Chapter Eight

Conclusion

My passion for the Eucharist was kindled in the 1960s in a convent chapel in London, where I was studying for my bachelor's degree at London University. When I visited the chapel, I was still a non-Catholic, and it was there that I discovered Christ present in the Eucharist. My passion for the poor began some twenty years later on the edge of a middle-class suburb of Dublin. Now a religious, I found a destitute woman in an empty room, lying on a bed without sheets or blankets, with no food and no heating. And it was just a few days before Christmas. Some twenty years later, on sabbatical in Georgetown University, I tried to bring these two loves together, and discovered an inseparable relationship between the Eucharist and the poor, and thus an exciting link between the Eucharist and social justice.

The Eucharist and social justice are not packaged separately. They come together. Hand in hand, they hold center stage. In its inherent unity and in the interlocking parts of its structure, the Eucharist is the source of solidarity with the oppressed and of nourishment for a commitment to social justice. It critically uncovers the injustices in today's society and provides both a spirituality for those engaged in social ministry for justice and a theological foundation for those who work with and for the poor.

Justice and "Different Moments" of the Eucharistic Celebration

I have traced the ethical implications of the Eucharist throughout "different moments" of its celebration in an attempt to discover how they critique some crucial social issues that characterize our fragmented society and the public discourse of our globalized world. Tracing the ethical implications of the Eucharist is also an attempt to decode "the potential of the parts of the Mass for developing our sense of justice."[1]

As we have seen, the Introductory Rite is essentially global and inclusive. From the very beginning of the celebration, the Eucharist is revealed as a sacrament of protest and resistance that requires us to stand with the oppressed. It is a vigorous critique of the exclusion strategies of economic globalization. The Penitential Rite immediately forges an unbreakable link between forgiveness and justice in the quest for peace. It is about the acknowledgment of individual wrongdoing and complicity in the social sin of oppression and injustice. It demands reconciliation as a strategy to break the cycles of violence that threaten world peace. The Liturgy of the Word underlines the connection between scripture readings and social injustices of our times. The Eucharist, like scripture, is full of humanitarian issues. Seated at the table of the Word of the just God, the God of all who suffer, we are challenged to incarnate justice and hold out hope to the oppressed. The Presentation of the Gifts embraces a whole host of contemporary, burning, social issues around the resources of the earth and basic human needs. With the gifts of bread and wine, the Presentation offers a foundation and paradigm for social action and the care of the planet.

The Eucharistic Prayer is a narrative in which the poor are both the priority and the reference point. Embedded in that prayer is the anamnestic memory of the suffering and the oppressed. The awe inspired by contemplating "the wonderful deeds of the Lord" erupts into an ethical compulsion to continue participation in the eucharistic celebration through solidarity with the poor in the practical spheres of life. The words of consecration—*This is my Body*—transform us. They adjust the lens through which we view the world, giving poverty a human face; they refocus our vision so as to see Christ in everyone, everywhere, especially in the vulnerable and disadvantaged. The eucharistic injunction to "do this in memory of me" initiates a dynamic strategy to reproduce the mission of Jesus Christ, who identified himself with the weak and the marginalized and who preached good news to the poor.

The Eucharist Is about Social Justice

Taken as a whole and unified event, the Eucharist transcends the specific liturgical action that makes it happen. There is a dynamic, organic relation between the Eucharist and both society and the world; a relationship that critiques the injustices inherent in that society and commits us to the poor of the world. In its very essence, the Eucharist is about social justice. Its power and its meaning can bring about a "eucharistic conversion" that empowers each one of us to stand in unity with the suffering and oppressed in the world.

The Eucharist Is about Real People

The Eucharist is about real people in the *real* world, not the world of extremists, religious or secular, nor that of dreamers. The Eucharist is alive with a vibrant relation to the existence and struggles of all men and women everywhere, especially the huge majority, the "two-thirds world" that is the poor. It has a historical dimension that revolves around issues of war and peace, liberty and despotism, development and poverty—affairs that find a prominent place on the world stage. The Eucharist does not deal in abstractions or generalities, ideas or concepts. It transcends the personal "inner feeling" that is incapable of protest in the society of exchange. It transcends the idealist mindset that impedes concern and action on behalf of the suffering worldwide. It has an eminently practical quality. It is totally relevant in a world where God has been distanced from the immediate circumstances of people's lives. It is about those lives, the lives of real people.

The Eucharist is not about statistics or percentages; rather, it embraces the enormous cultural, ethnic, and economic diversity of the planet, which is peopled by a kaleidoscope of billions of human faces and the hubbub of countless human voices, filtered through different languages, dialects, and accents. The Eucharist is truly "the world in a wafer"; a wafer "full of" black, white, brown, and yellow faces; faces of Christians, Muslims, Jews, Hindus, Buddhists, and of every believer and nonbeliever; faces of Africans, Europeans, and North Americans; faces from Asia, Oceania, Latin America, and the Caribbean; faces of those who have benefited from globalization and those who, most definitely, have not.

The Eucharist Is about Life

The Eucharist is about life and death, life *through* death. It is about the sacramental presence of the Risen Christ who died and rose that *we* might live. It is about the Risen Christ who transports the Last Supper into "forever" and transforms the bread broken and the wine poured out into life for the world. The eucharistic texts are replete with references to life:

CONCLUSION

The bread of life.[2]

Life giving bread.[3]

May this mingling of the body and blood of our Lord
Jesus bring eternal life to us who receive it.[4]

Rising you restored our life.[5]

As the bread of life, the Eucharist offers life for all in abun-
dance. It also gathers in all the justice issues around life and quality of life. It speaks to the life of the individual *and* the life of society. It links human life with human dignity. The Eucharist is a
meal, a symbol that expresses the hopes of the "two-thirds-world"
of the poor who are excluded by famine, illness, and war from the
world's banquet, but who are desperate to share the meal of life
with the rest of the world. The issue of global hunger leads beyond
the eucharistic table. The Eucharist challenges us to seek "a place at
the table of life for all God's children,"[6] especially for those unseated
from the table and robbed of their human dignity. The number of
those excluded from the banquet for various reasons increases in
number and degree. The poor and hungry look at the world across
a violent divide. Their lives are threatened daily, as they struggle to
exist in the face of famine, drought, natural disasters, sickness, and
war. They have a sense of being invaded, pillaged, and plundered
by conflict, too-often fueled by the arms trade.

The Eucharist raises our awareness, too, of the abuse of the
environment that threatens the life we all hold in common, especially the lives of the poor, who ironically contribute the least to the
exploitation and degradation of the planet. Eucharistic reverence
for the earth becomes an imperative toward a new sustainable way
of living together.

The Eucharist Is Global

The Eucharist is global. It provides a common language for all. It is a prophetic word spoken and celebrated "from east to west." The Eucharist acknowledges our common humanity. It is an action concerned with the "unity of the whole human race."[7] As such, it has the potential to act as a hermeneutical key to the complex and multifaceted reality called globalization. The Eucharist is a paradigm for all of us to understand ourselves as inhabitants of the global village: world citizens and members of a global civil society, concerned with the common good of humanity.

Because the Eucharist is essentially global, it embraces global issues. The international community has come to a deeper realization that some contemporary problems are global in nature and require global solutions. Some of those solutions are modeled by the Eucharist.

Today, marginalization on a global scale is growing. It has taken new forms and acquired new depth: discrimination, social exclusion, and inequality between "those on the margins" and those "at the center." The Eucharist imagines a different world; a world of an alternative global interconnectedness, based on dignity, respect, and equality, that reconfigures the pattern of global relationships in favor of all. The Eucharist transforms the web of global interconnectedness into a tapestry of solidarity that takes seriously the task of healing and reconciliation.

The Eucharist Is about Celebration

The Eucharist is a celebration, a toast to humanity. But, in a world of poverty amidst plenty, it is both a festive meal and a prophetic protest that challenges global hunger. A eucharistic imagination would see the Eucharist with its humanizing, global, and life-giving dimensions, as reflected in the "Carnival of the Oppressed" of the World Social Forum, which was celebrated in Kenya in 2007. It was a big, bright, colorful, and very loud grassroots meeting that brought the world to Africa. Coalitions and social movements from Asia, the Pacific, South America, the Caribbean, North America, Europe, and all corners of the African continent converged in Nairobi, for five days of celebration and resistance to injustice. It was a truly global gathering, committed, as is Eucharist, to social justice.

Among the themes were poverty and hunger, trade and the landless, migration and environmental damage: all issues that are encoded in the eucharistic celebration. The motto too, "Another World Is Possible," has a very eucharistic ring to it. Another world is possible, a different world, transformed because of the Eucharist. "The prayer which we repeat at every Mass. 'Give us this day our daily bread,' obliges us to do everything possible, in cooperation with international, state, and private institutions, to end or at least reduce the scandal of hunger and malnutrition afflicting so many millions of people in our world, especially in developing countries."[8] A better world is possible, in which "yesterday's bread" becomes "bread today," for all.

In my introduction, I posed some searching questions about the connection between the Eucharist and social justice. The answers are in the affirmative. Yes, the Eucharist is meant to reach beyond "the membership" to the whole world. Yes, it does have something to say about the impact that economic globalization has on the poor. Yes, the Eucharist does provide a theological basis for social justice. Yes, our eucharistic celebrations can overflow with a passion for justice and the poor.

Let's do it. We can make it happen.

Notes

1. Handmaids of the Sacred Heart of Jesus.

2. Cf. *Didascalia Apostolorum*: "The altar of the church are the poor, the widows, and the orphans." See also the writings of John Chrysostom, Irenaeus, and Basil.

3. St. Irenaeus, *Adv. Haereses*, IV, 18, 5: PG 7/1, 1028, quoted by Tony Kelly, CSsR, in "Suggestions towards a Eucharistic Ecology," in *Eucharist: Experience and Testimony*, ed. Tom Knowles, SSS (Melbourne, Australia: David Lovell Publishing, 2001), 84.

4. Make Poverty History campaign manifesto, www.makepovertyhistory.org.

5. Bob Geldof, launching Live 8, reported by BBC, www.bbc.co.uk/2/hi/entertainment.

6. *Time* Magazine, January 2, 2006.

7. Cf. *Washington Post*, "This year's Oscar goes to Social Issues," March 5, 2006.

8. Jeffrey Skoll, the billionaire cofounder of eBay, was convinced of the power of movies to change society and financed several movies with a social message: *North Country, Good Night and Good Luck,* and *Syriana*.

9. Francis Fukuyama, *America at the Crossroads: Democracy, Power, and the Neocon Legacy* (New Haven, CT: Yale University Press, 2006).

10. Francis Fukuyama, *The End of History and the Last Man* (New York: Free Press, 1992).

CHAPTER ONE

1. "Long live St. Romero of El Salvador! St. Romero of Latin America! St. Romero of the World!"

2. Manuel Diaz-Mateos, SJ, *Fruto de la tierra y trabajo de los hombres*, Separata No. 83, Paginas, May 1987. My translation.

3. *Lumen Gentium* 10.1.

4. Revised Edition of the *General Instruction of the Roman Missal*, 5, 69, 91 (2000).

5. Yves Congar, in *La Maison-Dieu*, n. 224, 109, quoted by David Orr, OSB, "The Exercise of the Priesthood of the Faithful in the Ritual of the Eucharist," in *Eucharist: Experience and Testimony*, ed. Tom Knowles, SSS (Melbourne, Australia: David Lovell Publishing, 2001), 186–95.

6. *Sacrosanctum Concilium* 14.

7. Tertullian, *On Prayer*, ch. xxvii.

8. Gen 1:29.

9. The Order of Mass, Eucharistic Prayer, in *The Sacramentary* (New York: Catholic Book Publishing Co., 1985), 372.

10. Alexander Schmemann, *Sacraments and Orthodoxy* (New York: Herder, 1965), 16. See Zizioulas, *Being as Communion*, passim.

11. Oscar Romero, radio broadcast homily, March 23, 1980.

12. Matt 5:6.

13. Pedro Casaldaliga, *Fuego y ceniza al viento*, Sal Terrae, Santander, 1984, 81.

14. John 4:32.

15. Luke 22:15.

16. Eucharistic Prayer IV, *The Sacramentary*, 557.

17. Ps 78:19.

18. Isa 25:6.

19. Mic 2:16.

20. Anne Thurston, "Corpus Christi," in *The Furrow*, vol. 44, No. 233, July–August 2005, 394.

21. Acts 4:32–35.

22. Joseph Cardinal Bernardin, quoted in *Living with Christ*, August 2005, 48.

23. Terence P. McCaughey, *Memory and Redemption*, Gill and McMillan, 1992.

24. William T. Cavanaugh, *The World in a Wafer: A Geography of the Eucharist as Resistance to Globalization*, 78.

25. Eucharistic Prayer III, *The Sacramentary*, 552.

26. John Paul II, *Mane Nobiscum Domine* 27.

27. Eucharistic Prayer III, *The Sacramentary*, 554.

28. Words of consecration in Eucharistic Prayers I, II, III, and IV.

29. Pablo Neruda, "Ode to Bread."

30. English, Spanish, Swahili.

31. See Hans-Georg Gadamer's "fusion of horizons" in *Truth and Method*, his major philosophical work, 1960. He posits that, in interpreting a text, a larger context gives meaning and a sense of perspective, broadening our horizons.

32. Kwame Gyeke, "Our One World: Thoughts on Globalization," in *Beyond Cultures: Perceiving a Common Humanity*, Ghanaian Philosophical Studies II. The J. B. Danquah Memorial Lectures, Ser. 32, Accra, 2002, 120.

33. *Pachamama* is the word in Quechua for "Mother Earth." The Incas of ancient Peru believed that *Pachamama* personified the Earth.

34. Rabindranath Tagore, at a dinner held in his honor in London, July 1912, quoted by Confluence Poetry, www.confluence.uk.net. Also quoted in Kofi A. Busia, *The Challenge of Africa* (New York: Frederick A. Praeger, 1962), 105.

35. Pascal Lamy, "Doha's Final Deadline," in *The World in 2007*, special issue of *The Economist*, 150.

36. John Simpson, "Summit will expose G8 fault lines," *Simpson's View*, July 4, 2005, BBC World News.

37. The U.S. government subsidizes rice growers at a cost to taxpayers of more than $1 billion a year. See "From Rice to Riches: Subsidies cost taxpayers billions," at www.taxpayer.net/agriculture/learnmore/factsheets/rice.pdf.

38. Cf. Andrew Maykuth, "Aid Hurting African Farmers," in *Philadelphia Inquirer*, June 30, 2005.

39. Kofi Annan, "Annan Urges G8 to Help Africa with Fairer Trade," press conference given in Sirte, Libya, at a meeting of the African Union, July 4, 2005. Reported by Reuters, http://today.reuters.com.news.

40. Andrew Rugasira, chief executive of Rwenzori, Ugandan coffee company, "G8 Business for Action for Africa Summit," London, July 5, 2005, BBC News, www.bbc.co.uk/2/hi/business/4653149.htm.

41. Larry Elliott, "Gordon Brown calls for overhaul of UN, World Bank and IMF," in *The Guardian*, January 18, 2007, 19.

42. Statistics reveal the following percentages of total voting power: United States, 16.38 percent; Brazil, 2.07 percent; Afghanistan, .03 percent. From the *World Bank Shareholders' Manual*, 2007.

43. A selection process adopted in October 2006 to nominate Mr. Ban Ki-moon of Korea as the new secretary-general, replacing Kofi Annan.

44. Cf. Paul Fahri, "Where the Rich and Elite Meet to Compete," in the *Washington Post*, February 5, 2006, 1.

45. Tony Blair, in keynote speech at the World Economic Forum, in Davos, Switzerland, January 26, 2005.

46. Ps 146:6c–7.

47. Deut 15:11–12.

48. A. Paoli, from some typewritten notes for a talk given in Medellín, Colombia, quoted by Dolores Aleixandre, *Siete verbos de acceso a la Eucaristia*, in Estudios, Sal Terrae, Santander, 1995, 340.

49. Michael Amaladoss, SJ, *Life in Freedom: Liberation Theologies from Asia* (Maryknoll, NY: Orbis, 1997), 30.

50. Cf. Naim Ateek's discussion on the inclusive character and nature of God, in *Justice and Only Justice* (Maryknoll, NY: Orbis Books, 1990), 92–100.

CHAPTER TWO

1. An Arabic word meaning "uprising." Here it refers to the second Palestinian uprising that broke out in September 2000 because of Israeli occupation.

2. Cf. Luis R. Negrón Hernández, *Kyrie Eléison, Christe Eléison, Origen histórico, significado, uso en la liturgia* ("Historical origin, meaning, use in the liturgy"), http://www.preb.com/amen/kyrie.htm.

3. Mark 10:46–7. See also Matt 9:27.

4. Matt 15:22.

5. Cf. Egeria's *Diary of a Pilgrimage*, where she describes the liturgical celebration in the Church of the resurrection in Jerusalem. *Diary of a Pilgrimage*, ed. George E. Gingas, Ancient Christian Writers (New York: Paulist Press, 1970).

6. "The Political Dimension of the Faith, based on an Option for the Poor," a speech given by Archbishop Romero at Louvain University, Belgium, on February 2, 1980, on receiving a doctorate *honoris causa*. "La dimensión política de la fe desde la opción por los pobres. Una experiencia eclesial en El Salvador, Centroamérica," http://www.servicioskoinonia.org/relat/135.htm.

7. Nelson Kirst, in *TEAR, Liturgia em revista*, vol. 1, n. 1, April 2000, www.selah.com.

8. Cf. *General Instruction of the Roman Missal*, 52.

9. Melissa Tuckey, poet and activist, quoted in *Sojourners*, February 2007.

10. Gerard Moore, SM, *Eucharist and Justice*, Catholic Social Justice Series (Sydney: Australian Catholic Social Justice Council, 2000), 10.

11. John Paul II, World Day of Peace, 2001, www.vatican.va/ holy_father/john_paul_ii/messages/peace/2001.

12. From the diary of Etty Hillesum, a Dutch Jew who survived Auschwitz, quoted by Marc Ellis in *Toward a Jewish Theology of Liberation: The Challenge of the 21st Century* (Maryknoll, NY: Orbis, 1987), 98, and by Naim Ateek, *Justice and Only Justice: A Palestinian Theology of Liberation* (Maryknoll, NY: Orbis, 1990), 186.

13. Statement by Cardinal Bertone, Vatican Secretary of State, September 16, 2006, www.vatican.va/roman_curia/secretariate _state/cardinal_bertone/2006/documents/20060916.

14. Marc H. Ellis, *Toward a Jewish Theology of Liberation: The Challenge of the 21st Century*, 3rd Expanded Edition (Waco, TX: Baylor University Press, 2004), 202.

15. Naim Stifan Ateek, *Justice and Only Justice: A Palestinian Theology of Liberation* (Maryknoll, NY: Orbis, 1989), 177.

16. *General Instruction of the Roman Missal*, 56, b., in *The Sacramentary* (New York: Catholic Book Publishing Co., 1985), 28–29.

17. Pope Benedict XVI, *Sacramentum Caritatis* 49, February 22, 2007, www.vatican.va/hf/ben-xvi.

18. Pope Paul VI, *Message for the Celebration of the Day of Peace*, January 1, 1972, www.vatican.va/hf/paul-vi.

19. Pope Benedict XVI, *Sacramentum Caritatis* 89.

20. Pope John Paul II, *Message for the Celebration of the XXX World Day of Peace*, January 1, 1997, www.vatican.va/holyfather/ john_paul_ii /messages/peace.

21. Pope Benedict XVI, *Sacramentum Caritatis* 89.

CHAPTER THREE

1. Luke 24:27.
2. "Today the Lord rose."
3. Luke 24:32.
4. Inhabitants of the *población*, or shanty town.

5. Paul Janowiak, quoted by David Orr, OSB, in "The Exercise of the Priesthood of the Faithful," in *Eucharist: Experience and Testimony*, ed. Tom Knowles, SSS (Melbourne, Australia: David Lovell Publishing, 2001), 101.

6. Philip Land, SJ, "Justice," in *The New Dictionary of Theology*, ed. Joseph A. Komonchak, Mary Collins, and Dermot A. Lane (Wilmington, DE: Michael Glazier, 1987), 548.

7. Deut 10:17–18. "The strangers" are sometimes referred to as the "resident alien." The English equivalent is "immigrant."

8. Mic 6:8.

9. Luke 4:18.

10. Walter J. Burghardt, *Justice: A Global Adventure* (Maryknoll, NY: Orbis, 2004), 12.

11. Genesis 2: the Y account of creation, which centers on man, as opposed to the priestly version in Genesis 1.

12. Cf. Alexander Schmemann, *For the Life of the World: Sacraments and Orthodoxy* (Crestwood, NY: St. Vladimir's Seminary Press, 1970), 10–16.

13. John R. Donahue, SJ, "What Does the Lord Require? A Bibliographical Essay on the Bible and Social Justice," *Studies in the Spirituality of Jesuits 25/2* (March 1993), 14.

14. Gen 22:18.

15. Exod 14:15—15:1.

16. Deut 24:17–18.

17. Deut 7:7–8.

18. See Walter J. Burghardt, *Justice: A Global Adventure*, (Maryknoll, NY: Orbis, 2004), 11.

19. First Reading Isa 54:5–14; Second Reading 55:1–11; Third Reading Bar 3:9–15, 32:44; Fourth Reading Ezek 36:16–17a, 18–28.

20. Isa 54:14.

21. Isa 55:1–2.

22. Bar 3:38.

23. Ibid 4:4.

24. Ezek 36:24.

25. Pope John Paul II, *Mane Nobiscum Domine* 27, www. vatican.va.

26. Sir 34:22.

27. Isa 1:11–16.

28. Hos 6:6.

29. Amos 5:23–24.

30. Isa 58:6–7.

31. Luke 20:47.

32. Cf. Mark 12:28–34.

33. Cf. Matt 23.

34. Matt 5:24.

35. Luke 21:1–4; also Mark 12:41–44.

36. 1 Cor 11:20–21.

37. Jas 1:27.

38. Deut 24:19.

39. John R. Donahue, SJ, op. cit., 3.

40. *General Introduction to the Lectionary*, 2nd ed. (Vatican: Sacred Congregation for the Sacraments and Divine Worship, 1981), 3.

41. *Sacrosanctum Concilium* 51, in *The Documents of Vatican II*, Walter Abbott, SJ (New York: The America Press, 1966), 155.

42. *Dei Verbum* 25, in Walter Abbott, SJ, op. cit., 127.

43. See *Gaudium et Spes* 43, in Walter Abbott, SJ, op. cit., 242–43.

44. See UN Food and Agricultural Organization Report, published November 22, 2005, Rome.

45. James D. Wolfensohn, *Annual World Bank Report*, 2004.

46. Eucharistic Prayer IV.

47. *Adv. Haereses*, 4, 18, 5: PG 7/1, 1028.

48. Jonathan Wolff and Avner de-Shalit, *Disadvantage*, Oxford Political Theory (New York: Oxford University Press, 2007).

49. John Paul II, *Mane Nobiscum Domine* 13.

50. Ibid., 28.

51. Michael Lerner, *The Left Hand of God* (San Francisco: HarperSanFrancisco, 2005), 5–6.

52. David Orr, op. cit., 191.

53. Luke 4:21.

54. *General Instruction of the Roman Missal*, 45.

55. Paul Janowiak, quoted by David Orr, OSB, "The Exercise of the Faithful in the Ritual of the Eucharist," *Eucharist, Experience and Testimony*, ed. Tom Knowles, SSS (Melbourne, Australia: David Lovell Publishing, 2001).

56. Isa 55:9–11.

57. *General Instruction of the Roman Missal*, 3.

58. *General Introduction to the Lectionary*, 9.

59. Thomas Merton, *The Wisdom of the Desert: Sayings from the Desert Fathers of the Fourth Century* (London: Hollis and Carter, 1961), 37.

Chapter Four

1. Ian Linden, *A New Map of the World* (London: Darton, Longman and Todd, 2003), ix.

2. Pope John Paul II, *Mane Nobiscum Domine* 27–28.

3. S. Painadath, SJ, "The Eucharist as the Sacrament of the Earth," in *Body, Bread, and Blood* (New Delhi: Vidyajyoti, 2003), 144.

4. See Pope Benedict XVI, *Sacramentum Caritatis* 47.

5. See St. Paul's vision of Christian life as a liturgy in Rom 12:1–2; Phil 2:17.

6. Presentation of the Gifts, *The Sacramentary* (New York: Catholic Book Publishing Co., 1985), 370–71.

7. Notably Bono and Bob Geldof, who have motivated other rock stars to participate in their worldwide concerts to reduce global poverty: Live Aid and Live 8.

8. Benjamín González Buelta, SJ, "Eucaristía, Pan producido," in *La utopia está ya en lo germinal*, Sal Terrae, Santander, 1998, 140–41. My translation.

9. Pablo Neruda, "Ode to Bread," in *Odas Elementales*, Editorial Seix, Barcelona, 1954, 19.

10. Pablo Neruda, "Ode to Wine," *Elementary Odes*, http://sunsite.dcc.chile.cl/chile/misc/odas.html.

11. The movie *Maria Full of Grace* tells Maria Alvarez's story, www.mariafullofgrace.com.

12. Pope Benedict XVI, *Sacramentum Caritatis* 47.

13. *The Cappuccino Trail*, BBC, 2001.

14. EU average production costs are more than double the production costs in countries like Brazil or Zambia.

15. Jo Leadbeater, head of Oxfam International's EU Advocacy Office. Press release, April 14, 2004, www.oxfam.org/eng/pr040414_trade_sugar_eu.htm.

16. See *World Water Crisis: Dawn of a Thirsty Century*, BBC World, June 2, 2000.

17. Benjamín González Buelta, SJ, op. cit., 142–43.

18. Isa 5:8.

19. Gerard Moore, SM, *Eucharist and Justice*, Catholic Social Justice Series (Sydney: Australian Catholic Social Justice Council, 2000), 20.

20. Interview with Ruben Shakay, Achuar Indian Guide, Kapawi Ecolodge, Ecuador, BBC World News, May 4, 2005.

21. BBC World News, November 10, 2004.

22. See Pope John Paul II, *Laborem Exercens* 21.

23. Presentation of the Gifts, *The Sacramentary*, 371.

24. Matt 11:25.

25. John 1:2–3.

26. Col 1:16.

27. Pablo Neruda, "Ode to Bread."

28. St. Irenaeus, *Adv. Haereses*, 5.2.2.

29. Steve Connor, "How a century of destruction has laid bare the world's rainforests," in *The Independent*, Saturday, July 10, 2004.

30. Leonardo Boff, *Cry of the Earth, Cry of the Poor* (Maryknoll, NY: Orbis, 1997), 110.

31. *National Catholic Reporter*, October 6, 2005.

32. Gerard Moore, SM, *Eucharist and Justice*, Catholic Social Justice Series (Sydney: Australian Catholic Social Justice Council, 2000), 17–18.

33. Teilhard de Chardin, *Hymn of the Universe* (New York: Harper and Row, 1961), 19.

34. See 1 Cor 16:2, Rom 15:26–28, Gal 2:10, 2 Cor 8–9.

35. Pedro Casaldaliga, *Fuego y ceniza al viento*, Sal Terrae, Santander, 1984, 41.

CHAPTER FIVE

1. Bono, foreword to Jeffrey Sachs's *The End of Poverty: Economic Possibilities for the Future* (New York: Penguin Press, 2005), xviii.

2. Here I am following a holistic approach to the Eucharistic Prayer, positing a close linkage between the Memorial Prayer, during which we give thanks, and the anamnesis proper, giving an anamnestic nature to the whole anaphora as a "memorial proclamation of the salvific works of God." Cf. David Power, "The Anamnesis: Remembering, We Offer," in *New Eucharistic Prayers: An Ecumenical Study of Their Development and Structure*, ed. Frank C. Senn (New York: Paulist Press, 1987). Cf. also Josep M.ª Rovira Belloso, *Un Senor, una mesa compartida, un envio al mundo*, in Sal Terrae, Santander, 1999.

3. Isa 49:15. See also Isa 44:21.

4. Luke 1:68–73.

5. Bartolomé de las Casas, *Carta al Concejo*, 1531, O.W. 44b, quoted by Gustavo Gutiérrez, *Las Casas*, in *Search of the Poor of Jesus Christ*, trans. Robert R. Barr (Maryknoll, NY: Orbis, 1993), 61, 194, 459.

6. Bartolomé de Las Casas, *Doce dudas*, 1564, O.E. 5:512b; quoted by Gutiérrez, op. cit., 18.

7. John 3:16.

8. Gustavo Gutiérrez, op. cit., 18.

9. Gustavo Gutiérrez, op. cit., 63.

10. See Matt 25:35–46.

11. Pope Paul VI, *Address during Last General Meeting of the Second Vatican Council*, December 7, 1965, www.vatican.va.

12. The women who live in the *poblaciones*, or shanty towns, in South America.

13. Ps 107:8–9.

14. Eucharistic Prayer IV, *The Sacramentary* (New York: Catholic Book Publishing Co., 1985), 556.

15. Metz, J. B., *Glaube in Geschichte und Gesellschaft*, Mainz, 1967, 76–180, quoted by Cyriac Vazhayil, OFM Cap, in *Body, Bread, Blood*, Delhi, 2000, 286.

16. See the Beatitudes, Matt 5:8.

17. Memorial Prayer, Eucharistic Prayer I, *The Sacramentary* (New York: Catholic Publishing Co., 1985), 546.

18. Phil 2:7–8.

19. Luke 3:22.

20. Margaret Silf, *Sacred Spaces* (Oxford: Lion Publishing, 2001), 33.

21. Mal 3:5.

22. Eucharistic Prayer IV, *The Sacramentary*, 577.

23. Eucharistic Prayer II, *The Sacramentary*, 548–50.

24. Bruce T. Morrill, SJ, *Anamnesis as Dangerous Memory: A Dialogue Between Liturgical and Political Theology*, 9, http://fm www. bc.edu/SJ/morrill.html.

25. Robert Gascoigne, "The Eucharist and Ethics," in *Eucharist: Experience and Testimony*, ed. Tom Knowles, SSS (Melbourne, Australia: David Lovell Publishing, 2001), 108.

26. Modern theologians like Johann B. Metz speak of a "memory of the future."

27. John 12:24.

28. Native peoples and those who work on the land.

29. St. Ignatius of Loyola, *Spiritual Exercises* [195], Introducción, texto, notas y vocubulario por Cándido Dalmases, SJ, Sal Terrae, Santander, 1987, 120. My translation.

30. Pope John Paul II, *Tertio Millennio Adveniente* 37, www.vatican.va. Italics are in the original.

31. St. Thomas Aquinas, in *Ep. Ad Rom., c.8, lect.7*: "Patitur etiam propter Christum non solum qui patitur propter fidem Christi, sed etaim qui patitur pro quocumque justitiae opera amore Christi." See also *Summa Theologica, II–II q.124, ad 3*.

32. From an audio recording of Archbishop Romero's last Mass, played during the celebration of the 25th anniversary of his death, April 1, 2005, at the University of Central America. My translation. The shot that killed Romero is also recorded on the audio tape.

33. See 1 Cor 11:17–34.

34. Kevin Merida and Michael A. Fletcher, "For the Poor, Sudden Celebrity," *Washington Post*, September 22, 2005, A-1.

35. Gerard Moore, SM, *Eucharist and Justice*, Catholic Social Justice Series (Sydney: Australian Catholic Social Justice Council, 2000), 17.

36. Jas 2:15.

37. Martin Luther King, "I have a dream," a speech delivered on the steps of the Lincoln Memorial, Washington, DC, August 28, 1963.

38. Bruce T. Morrill, op. cit., 1, 8.

39. Pedro Casaldaliga, *Todavia estas Palabras, A Bartolomé de Las Casas*, www.servicioskoinonia.org-pedro-poesia-todaviae.htm.

CHAPTER SIX

1. Pedro Lamet, SJ, *Este es mi Cuerpo*, PPC Editorial, Madrid, 1995.

2. See Bob Geldof, "Starting to make poverty history," in *The World in 2006*, special issue of *The Economist*, 89.

3. See UN report, *Trafficking in Persons: Global Patterns, 2006*.

4. Deborah Orr, "Sex, Slavery and the Scandal of a Trade in Women that Shames the Whole World," in *The Independent*, April 26, 2006, 39.

5. Eucharistic Prayer II, *The Sacramentary*, 548.

6. Eucharistic Prayer IV, *The Sacramentary*, 558.

7. Eucharistic Prayer III, *The Sacramentary*, 552.

8. Ibid.

9. See Luke 24:13–35.

10. Memorial Acclamation 1, *The Sacramentary*, 545.

11. Christ is present in the Eucharist in different ways: in the people assembled, in the Word proclaimed, and in the Body and Blood shared.

12. Herbert McCabe, OP, "The Eucharist as Language," in *Catholicism and Catholicity: Eucharistic Communities in Historical and Contemporary Perspectives*, ed. Sarah Beckwith (Oxford: Blackwell, 1999), 19–29.

13. *Eucharistic Prayer for Masses for Various Needs and Occasions* (Totowa, NJ: Catholic Book Publishing Co., 1996), 49.

14. See www.un.org/millenniumgoals.

15. St. Augustine, Sermon 228B, in *Sermons 184–229Z*, trans. Edmund Hill, OP, Works of St. Augustine in Translation (Hyde Park, NY: New City Press, 2002), 262.

16. See Matt 25:31–46.

17. Acts 9:1–5.

18. See St. John Chrysostom, *Homily 20, 2 Cor 9:10*. Nicene and Post-Nicene Fathers Series, vol. 12, 115. Quoted by Carmel Pilcher, RSJ, "Eucharist and Life in John Chrysostom" in *Eucharist: Experience and Testimony*, ed. Tom Knowles (Melbourne, Australia: David Lovell Publishing, 2001), 215.

19. See Angela of Foligno, *Memorial*, V, 122–40.

20. In Chile, the elderly are affectionately referred to as "Grandpa" and "Grandma."

21. 1 Cor 10:17.

22. Eucharistic Prayer IV, *The Sacramentary*, 558–59.

23. 1 Cor 12:12.

24. Works of St. Augustine in Translation, op. cit., 265–66.

25. 1 Cor 12:26.

26. 1 Cor 12:22.

27. Samuel Ryan, "Asia and Justice," in *Vidyajyoti*, 1986, 357–58.

28. Such an understanding does not imply a form of pantheism but rather, the recognition of the reality of the incarnation. Cf. "The Incarnation means that the Son of God has bent over creation, made in, through and for him, saying, 'This is my Body,'" Samuel Ryan, "My Body for You," *Body, Bread, Blood: Eucharistic Perspectives from the Indian Church* (Delhi: Cambridge Press, 2000), 209.

29. Teilhard de Chardin, *The Mass on the World*, quoted by Thomas M. King, SJ, *Teilhard's Mass* (Mahwah, NJ: Paulist Press, 2005), 158.

30. Ibid., 148.

31. Samuel Ryan, "Body for You," 208.

32. See Rom 8:19–23.

33. Col 1:17.

34. Michael Himes, *Doing the Truth in Love: Conversations about God, Relationships, and Service* (Mahwah, NJ: Paulist Press, 1999), 129.

35. Eucharistic Prayer IV, *The Sacramentary*, 560.

36. Christian Aid Report, "The Climate of Poverty: Facts, Fears and Hope," May 2006, www.christian-aid.org.uk.

37. Teilhard de Chardin, *Mass on the World*, quoted by Thomas M. King, SJ, *Teilhard's Mass* (Mahwah, NJ: Paulist Press, 2005), 148.

38. Wendell Berry, *The Gift of Good Land* (San Francisco: North Point Press, 1981), 281.

39. Anne Penketh, "Aids and a lost generation," *The Independent*, May 16, 2004, 2.

40. See Oliver Conway, "U.S. capital faces 'serious' HIV challenge," BBC News, December 1, 2005.

41. See references to Teilhard de Chardin, "Este es mi Cuerpo," and Samuel Ryan in the text.

42. Text of the Eucharistic Consecration, *The Sacramentary*, 545.

Chapter Seven

1. Eucharistic Prayer IV, *The Sacramentary*, 557.

2. Pope John Paul II, *Mane Nobiscum Domine* 28.

3. See 1 Cor 11:17–34. See also St. Ignatius of Antioch, Letter to the Smyrnaeans, 6–7. Quoted by William T. Cavanagh, *Torture and the Eucharist* (Malden, MA: Blackwell Publishers, 1998), 231.

4. Pratibha Thaker, "Africa: Hope or Hype," in *The World in 2006*, special issue of *The Economist*, 2006, 87–88.

5. Jeffrey D. Sachs, in *Time* magazine, March 14, 2005.

6. The Fifty-Ninth World Health Assembly, May 22–27, 2006, in Geneva, Switzerland, www.who.int/en.

7. See "God's Politics Blog," by Jim Wallis and friends, *Sojourners*, January 29, 2007.

8. www.itto.or.jp.

9. Kofi Annan, *Investing in Development*, 2006, n. 221.

10. Kofi Annan, *In Larger Freedom*, 2006, n. 23.

11. Paul Wolfowitz, in *The World in 2006*, special issue of *The Economist*, 2006, 146.

12. Madeleine Albright, *The Mighty and the Almighty* (New York: Harper Collins, 2006), 50–51.

13. Kofi Annan, *In Larger Freedom*, n. 221.

14. *Marie Claire* magazine, June 2005, 38, reprinted from *Bono in Conversation with Michka Assaya*, Penguin Books, New York.

15. Ibid.

16. Global hunger statistics taken from *www.globalissues.org*.

17. Acts 2:44–47 and 4:34–35.

18. Samuel Ryan, SJ, "My Body for You," in *Body, Bread, Blood*, New Delhi, 2000, 204.

19. See Mark 6:37.

20. Eucharistic Prayer for a Mass of Reconciliation II, *The Sacramentary*, 1132.

21. Astrid Lobo Gajiwala, "The Passion of the Womb: Women Re-living the Eucharist," in *Body, Bread, Blood*, New Delhi, 2000, 120.

22. Luke 22:19.

23. See Mark 1:37.

24. Mark 6:31. See also Mark 3:20.

25. Eucharistic Prayer II, *The Sacramentary*, 548.

26. See William T. Cavanagh, *Torture and the Eucharist* (Malden, MA: Blackwell Publishers, 1998). He opines that the Eucharist was the Church's answer to torture under the military dictatorship of Pinochet in Chile.

27. Quoted in *Salvanet*, March–April 2000, 3, www.crispaz. org/news/net/2000/0200.pdf.

28. See Mark 6:30–44; Luke 9:10–17.

29. Michael Lerner, *The Left Hand of God*, HarperSan Francisco, 2005, 358.

30. Jonathan Sacks, *The Dignity of Difference*, Continuum, London, 2002, 23.

31. Phil 2:5.

32. Madeleine Albright, op. cit., 99.

33. See John 13:15.

34. Mark 5:43.

35. John 6:35.

36. Luke 10:21.

37. See Matt 25:31–46.

38. John 1:14.

39. See Micah 6:8.

40. See Luke 7:22.

41. Luke 10:29–36.

42. Doxology, *The Sacramentary*, 547.

43. Pedro Casaldaliga, "Todavía estas palabras," Estella, 1989, 80. My translation.

44. Raimundo Pannikar, "Man as a Ritual Being," *Chicago Studies* 16, 1977: 27.

Chapter Eight

1. Gerard Moore, SM, op. cit., Foreword, 5.

2. Memorial Prayer, Eucharistic Prayer I, *The Sacramentary* (New York: Catholic Book Publishing Co., 1985), 546.

3. Ibid., Memorial Prayer, Eucharistic Prayer II, 550.

4. Ibid., Breaking of the Bread, 563.

5. Ibid., Memorial Acclamation B, 545.

6. Pastoral reflection of United States Conference of Bishops, USCCB, *A Place at the Table*, November 13, 2002.

7. Pope John Paul II, *Mane Nobiscum Domine* 27.

8. Pope Benedict XVI, *Sacramentum Caritatis* 91.